THE MYSTIC TRUMPETER

THE
MYSTIC
TRUMPETER

JERRY MARSHALL
(MARSHALL JEROME ROSENKRANTZ)

𝓑LUE HAIR LADY

THE MYSTIC TRUMPETER

Copyright © 2012 by Jerry Marshall

Published by Blue Hair Lady Publishing
Miami, Florida 33155

www.bluehairlady.com
laura@lauracerwinske.com

Cover Art by Barry Zaid

DEDICATION

I dedicate this book to my wife Gail,
my soul mate and savior,
whose abundant love, patience, and
support enabled this work to be.

This book is not a doctrine of faith nor a guideline for a journey through the "The Dark Night of the Soul."

It is simply a well- documented and thoroughly honest account of a spiritual quest.

My guides have told me:

You are Our trumpeter
and through you we hope to
"blow down the walls"
of mankind's minds
and replace those "walls"
with direct and open lines,
all parallel,
that meet in God!

The trumpet is the universal instrument
of announcement, of arrival.

In my own life,
it was the instrument
of my earthly deliverance.

With this book,
I trumpet my "spiritual revival."

CONTENTS

PREFACE

STORY OF A DEVOTION

You must get done with the blog and the book!
They are essential at this moment!
All that you have on your computer is of
utmost value, and if I had to compare it,
it would be by describing the lost jars in
the desert that filled in so many gaps.

It doesn't matter who gets the message!
It simply matters that it is gotten out in a universe run amuck!

THE MESSAGE ABOVE CAME TO Jerry Marshall in the spring of 2008, 15 years after the first channeling occurred and six years after he and I began formulating this book. Over the course of those years I witnessed Jerry's inspiration and desolation as he continuously struggled with his mission, delighting in it and doubting it, honoring it and anguishing over how to get these words out to the world. His fundamental question was, "Why me?" Among the many "crosses" the process caused him to bear was that of finding others with whom he could share his experience. When, for example, he confided his fears over exposing his calling to a psychiatrist at the V.A. hospital, the doctor promptly classified him as schizophrenic. Close friends with whom he shared his insights listened respectfully, but seldom grasped the depth or demands of his commitment. He spoke to small groups of other mystically minded individuals and engaged over the internet for a while with a circle of channelers who also received messages from John Lennon. In the end, it was his abject, solitary perseverance – and his wife Gail's deeply tested patience – that brought the book about.

During this period, Jerry, being an artist, also produced other inspired works that reflected the meaning of his channelings. He wrote plays and composed a powerful piece for jazz orchestra based on Walt Whitman's poem, "The Mystic Trumpet". As a student of spiritual practice for more than 35 years, I have encountered all manner of reports of divine experience. But I must admit even I was skeptical when Jerry first mentioned his relationship with John Lennon – and this was before learning of his channelings of Onan from Neptune, Pope John II, and Jesus Christ. But never once, for even a moment, did I doubt the veracity of Jerry's experience. Every word he recorded perfectly aligned with all I had learned in my decades of spiritual exploration. And every word was an inspiration, often hard won. In addition to his great humor, musical gifts, and warm personality, Jerry also has a darker side. When the agony of where to turn and how to disseminate his message grew overwhelming, he often slid in to depression or a paralysis of confusion and doubt. Inevitably, however, Spirit returned to answer his perennial question, "Why me, Lord?" And that answer was always direct and simple: "Because you're listening."

In July of 1998, Jerry channeled these words:

Yes, it is I, God, in answer to your prayer of yesterday. Nothing goes unheard. You cried out in anguish, and your cry was heard. Could you ever have imagined that you would be sitting in conversation with ME one on one? Yet here We are and you can't allow yourself the pleasure…. You still can't accept your hard-earned gift. How many people on earth do you think enjoy this privilege? Yet you still can't enjoy it. You have worked for this moment all of your soul's existence! Why You?! Why not!? You can't know of all your past incarnations, and so you can't see the great wall you have climbed. But We can! It's a painting on Our walls, and it's about to be signed, if you can but find the courage to come and play with Us. The gift is in your hands and just waiting to be opened. You are fully worthy. Share it. Spread it around. Let people know the heights to which they can aspire. It's all available and available to all. It is a glorious sight. You would love to see what it is that We see.

Laura Cerwinske
Miami, FL
January 22, 2012

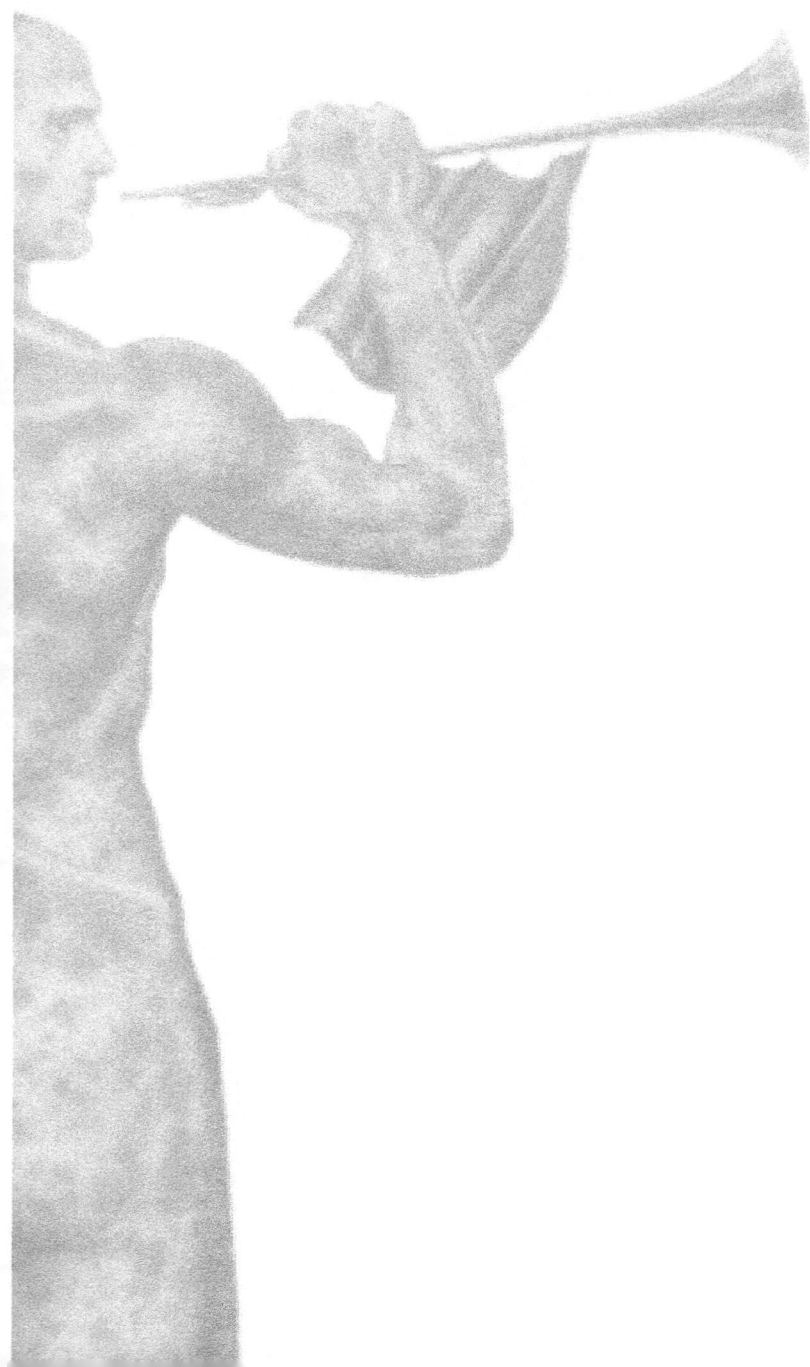

INTRODUCTION

HOW THE VOICES OF SPIRIT
FIRST ENTERED MY LIFE

*W*HAT HAPPENS WHEN A NICE Jewish horn player from the Bronx starts hearing voices – those of God, Jesus, the Pope, Onan – the spiritual incarnation of Gurdjieff – and, no less, John Lennon! Does he believe himself to be mad, as medical doctors would tell him, or does he battle his doubts and torment in order to listen and learn? Jerry Marshall's continuous questions was always, "Why me?"

Here is how his story began:

In the early 1980s I received a Transcendental Meditation mantra. My practice was to sit in a chair in my room and recite the mantra. My purpose was purely to quiet the mind, to free myself from the agitation and distraction that overpowered me. Not only did I have no interest in channeling, I had no idea about it.

Then, one day in 1993, I was in an otherwise empty train car on my way to a screenwriting course in downtown Miami when I heard a voice and looked around. No one else was on the train. Having read many spiritually oriented books, I wondered if I was having some kind of mystical experience. "I can't handle this right now," I thought. But I swore to myself that when I got home, I would sit and meditate. I did, and the words kept coming.

The voice revealed itself to be a guide named Onan:

You are involved in a process as old as time (time, that is, in your concept). It is definitely nothing new, except to your consciousness. As you become more and more aware, you will drop the barriers to our presence and allow a discourse which can only have illuminating effects on your universe.

I am Onan and I have been your spiritual guide through many incarnations. I have found you to be easy and likeable, but hard of head. That seems to have eased of late.

There are many things I wish to discuss with you and this is a very good time for us to do it.

My immediate reaction was amazement. How could this complete stranger know all this about me and articulate it so convincingly? Somehow my mind accommodated the moment and I asked: What is the most important action I must take in order to fulfill my mission here on earth?

First, you must put your house in order. Not that you are leaving that soon, but your disorder keeps us from having this kind of time together.

You must learn to develop disciplined work habits and allot a proper amount of time for each project.

You are already fulfilling that mission by speaking and acting in such a manner as to spread the word. Each ripple becomes like a wave when the ocean begins to move inexorably towards its distant shore. We are your distant shore and will welcome you home when it's your time! For now, continue along your path and keep in touch, Onan

IN THE BEGINNING
JANUARY, 1941

I was eleven years old when I saw my father for the last time. Our family – Dad, Mother, my younger brother Stan, and I – lived in a 3rd floor walk-up in the Bronx. Dad was sitting in his chair when the pain struck. The ambulance took him away, chair and all. The next thing I knew, my whole world had changed.

For days, our apartment was filled with relatives who came for the *shiva* (the traditional Jewish mourning). Among them was my father's brother, a plumber from Brooklyn. Uncle Mike belonged to an American Legion post that had a drum and bugle corps. I barely knew the man. He barely knew me. For some reason, he came to the *shiva* with a trumpet for me and an offer to play in his post's drum and bugle corps. Fleeing the emotional torrent of the *shiva*, I took the instrument into the bedroom. From the first breath, I instinctively knew how to make musical sounds on it, while never dreaming it would become my salvation.

I played all the time, in between school and my job delivering for the neighborhood butcher. At night, I'd sit in the dark and play to the Nat King Cole or Sinatra tunes on the radio. On weekends I played at school dances and parties. I joined the musicians' union at age fifteen!

When I was sixteen, I went on a date with a lovely Gentile girl from my neighborhood. Of course, because she wasn't Jewish, I couldn't tell my mother, and the secrecy made the date all the more exciting. She asked to see *The Red Shoes*, a ballet film which I had absolutely no interest in watching. But if this was what she liked….

To my enormous wonder, the film mesmerized me. I'd never before experienced sound and color as pure sensation. For the first time, I was seeing the way artists see. Not that I thought of myself as an artist. But this was the first time I thought about what it meant to be the one.

In 1945, I became the trumpeter for the Bob Leyton Band, which toured the Midwest. During those endless road trips, I occupied myself by reading. Like the trumpet, one of these books changed my life: Somerset Maughm's *The Razor's Edge* offered my first glimpse into spirit.

After returning from military service in Korea in 1959, I joined the Charlie Barnett band and ended up playing at Martha Raye's 5 O'Clock Club on Miami Beach. It was a dream job and a stepping stone to even better ones. Eventually I became Music Director at the swankiest hotels on Miami Beach during their heyday in the 1960's: the Fountainebleu, the Diplomat, and the Eden Roc. I was fortunate to play for and with such musical luminaries as Frank Sinatra, Lena Horne, Tony Bennett, Jackie Gleason, and others. The money was great, and the work was steady, but my life was a frantic schedule of rehearsals, convention dates and gala social events. Being in total denial of my artistic and spiritual needs, I experienced my success as no more than a pressure cooker of fear and rage. If one of the musicians came to a job wearing white, instead of dark, socks, I'd erupt as if he carried pox. If a musician played sitting down, I'd berate him as if he'd ruined a symphonic debut. My life was hardly the joyous and exuberant as my musical perfomances made it appear. I looked on my career not as a gift, but strictly as a way to make a living. Music was my job.

My conscious journey toward a knowlege of spirit began with my work with Dr. Syril Marquit, a psychologist, who, throughout the late 1950s and sixties, taught me how to examine – and discard, if necessary – the darker aspects of my mind. For the following twenty years, Dr. William Leone, a psychiatrist, worked with me in opening the well of my buried emotions. In the late 1970s, I unintentionally found myself at the Edgar Cayce Institute, Association for Research and Enlightenment where my decidedly anti-mystical attitudes began to crumble. The denouement came when I was introduced, a year later, to *A Course in Miracles*. A profound teaching in self-awareness, channeled by, of all things, a Columbia University psychiatry professor, the course fostered my understanding of how all perception is projection. Later, I began studying with a teacher named Malaila (now known as Ysatis) who guided me in reading, meditating, listening more carefully, and observing my thoughts. I became emotionally quieter.

HOW I EXPERIENCE SPIRIT

One year after that initial channeling, the one that came unbidden on the train, I began receiving lessons on the workings of quantum physics and of my/our role in the universe from a voice that identified itself as the Holy Spirit. A year after that, during a channeling in which Onan was speaking, he quite unexpectedly advised me to, "Stand by for Lenin," or at least that's what I thought he was saying. But it proved to be Lennon, John Lennon, who wished to speak to me, and it was he who would, over the next many years, convey to me the understanding that each spirit who comes to me is, in fact, an ethereal embodiment of "all my loving guides."

When I meditate, my initial intent is to simply quiet my mind and listen. As a result, countless avenues open to all of my spiritual guides. As they speak to me, I write everything down, later transcribing their words to my computer. Throughout the day I try to incorporate their messages into my life.

Whenever I get caught up in the past or the future, in fear or desire, anger or greed, I am lost to Spirit, which is to say, to my own Higher Self. My guides have inspired in me the belief that this "life" is an illusion, a sleeping dream that disappears upon waking. My intention and attention keep me centered on my Spirit consciousness!.

All that Spirit requires of me is to awaken to Love and fulfill my part in the Divine plan. I count my blessings and try to maintain a thought of Spirit throughout the many aspects of my daily life. I recognize now that anyone who wants a deeper relationship with Spirit need only let the wanting become the most important element in his or her being.

Other communications came from deceased loved ones, including my brother Stan and his son Matthew, who died at the age of 15; my father Murray, my mother Betty; and my former wife. I would receive channelings from "All," who instructed me as to how, "There is no separation among us." Often I would hear from my "Guides Too Numerous to Mention."

When Jesus came through, I was baffled. What could I possibly understand of the Christian Lord. Yet, He knew me so well:

All is in place for your future activities on our behalf if you simply can get out of the way with your hard head! It is a miracle and a testimony to your desire that you have been able to scale these heights and we are much appreciative, for you have the ability and consciousness to spread the "Truth" wherever you are. It is best by example, and your demeanor of late easily speaks to the level of your concentration, desire,, dedication, devotion and as many other (adverbs) necessary to describe your commitment top growth.

Keep up the good fight! You are surrounded by love on all sides, and you are safe in the arms of the Lord. I am only a thought away at any moment and anxious to guide you through the channels now open to you. Use us freely and we will be there, or here, for you at a moment's notice.

This is a time of renewal. Just as a farmer must sow his fields before each planting, so it is with the earth at present. All of the soil has to be tilled and fertilized with a new consciousness, and that cannot be done while there are so many contaminants keeping it in constant turmoil.

Either you do it or Nature, which is all of us souls wishing to preserve our playgrounds, will do it for you. Remember, the first and foremost reality is that you all are souls, and the only difference is your degree of consciousness.

CHANNELING JOHN LENNON

I hated John Lennon's music.

As a musician, arranger, composer, and musical director, I considered his to be below even a basic level, and I thought the lyrics infantile. Also, to my mind, eyes, and ears, his 1960s mode of living seemed insane. But those were the time, and, of course, Beatles songs were often requested at our engagements. My job was to provide entertainment, so when someone wanted to hear a Beatles tune, I would simply turn to my guitar player and let him loose. It worked for my band and the party, and knowing what would work was my job. Musically, however, playing Beatles music was torture for me. After all the years of studying trumpet, playing and singing, I had ended up as a tambourine player!

Sometime during the 1980s a bride, while planning her wedding reception, requested the Beatles song Here, There, and Everywhere for her first dance. I had never heard it before, but having dutifully bought along a Beatles songbook, I performed it. But the end, I realized I had been missing out on a cultural phenonmenon. Soon I was reading everything I could about the Beatles' journey and influences and being reminded of my own epiphanies.

Thus, during a channeling in the 1990s my mind was open for what was about to become a beautiful friendship with John

"Suppose we try an experiment," he said to me one morning. "I will try to hum a few bars of a melody and then imply a lyric idea on my current experiences. I'm not sure how this process will work, but surely if I can access you logical mind over your ego's short circuitry, there must be a way of imprinting other types of information. I will begin by imagining my guitar and the best reference will be the E string. I'll dictate random intervals and you write them down. I'll be able to ascertain if they are correct without any trouble. It would be too hard to explain how I'm able to do this. Let's go!"

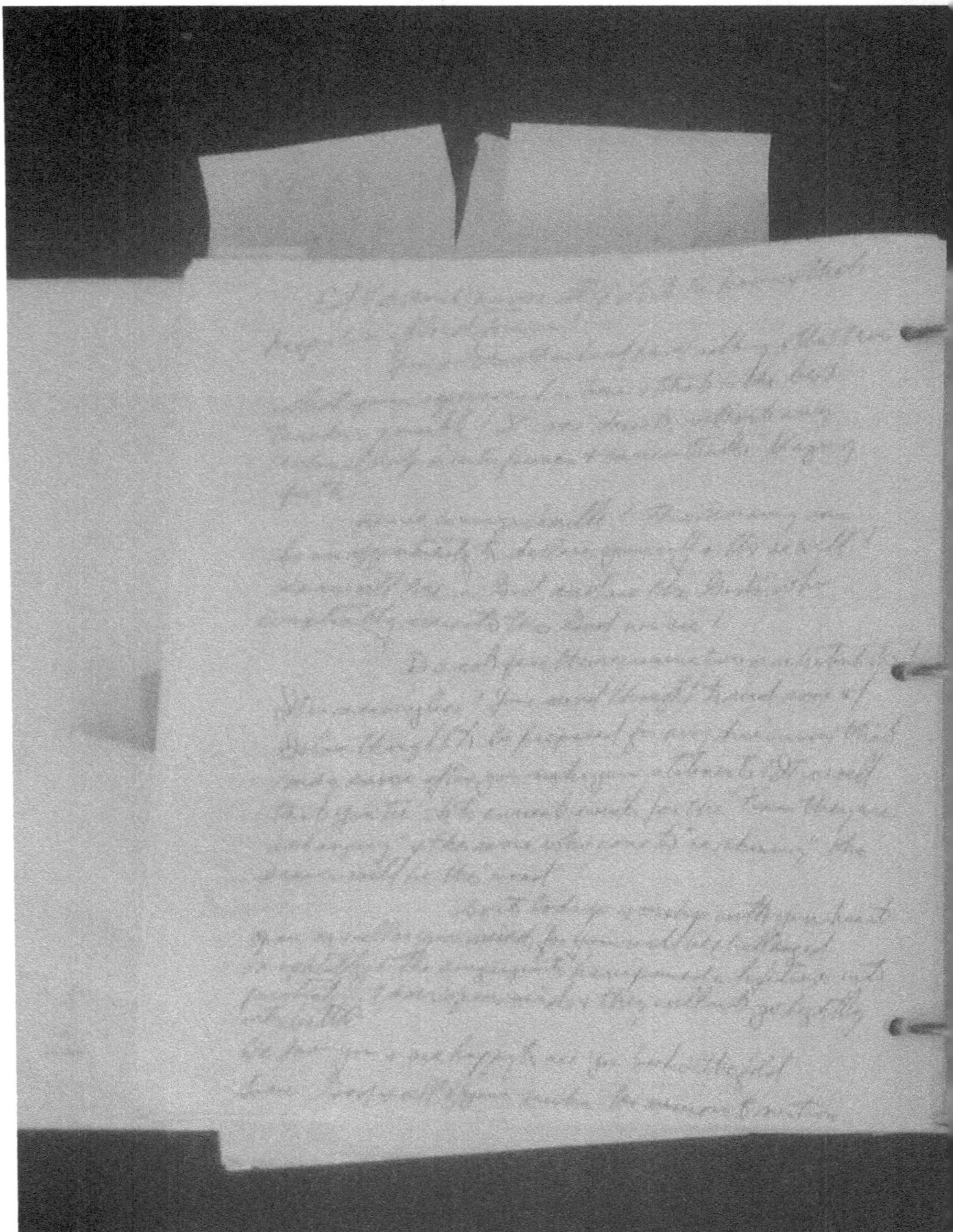

10/28/03 Tuesday   8 A.M.
Sinking lower and lower! Gail and I am _____ are speaking
to each other from 2 separated realitie _____ per in
despair! I have no desire to rejoin the _____ I could
gladly get on an ice flow and rejoin the endless ocean.

Sit quietly and listen! Sure, you can write it all down.

You hear Gail and she speaks truth! Locking yourself in your room is a death
sentence! You hang by a thread and she is that thread! All others in your "real" life
are busy with their own lives and that is as it should be! You, however, have no way
to reach out since your fears overpower you at every turn!

What have you to fear! We have given you the keys to the kingdom and you stay
locked in the cellar! Poke your head out and smell the air! It's safe out "there" for
you are surrounded by Our love! It is no accident that Rey would lead you to Ruben
(Perczek, Unitarian meeting)! There is a feeling ground and each is equipped with
information the other needs! The beauty is that there is no "other"! You know it
intellectually and even grasp the significance of the spiritual nature of it, but it is as
your mother was in Moodus, Conn. sitting on Golden Pond and suffering inside so that
she couldn't see the beauty surrounding her! You see the beauty surrounding you;
the sweetness of Gail's coming back to kiss you goodbye, and you even commented
on how lovely she looks, and yet you are stuck in your hell of your own creation!

It is brilliant! It holds all of your past, and even your future if you like, in one
container! Cluttered by so much of who you were that you can't see who you are!
You are Our representative on Planet Earth and you have an awesome responsibility,
ever since you accepted the mantle, to do Our work here on Earth!

Create some quotes that will encourage Ruben to join you in your efforts! He is well
equipped! He is in a different place than you are in his sojourn! Family
responsibilities weigh heavy in his decisions as to his time devoted to Dollars. Appeal
to him from that standpoint! Perhaps a partner in the venture so that it would put
him into a larger framework! It's worth a try!

You have been aware of Peak Performance since early college (psychology professor,
wrestling coach, art gallery owner). Maslow is no stranger to you! It is now time for
your peak performance! You have had many other peak performances over your
years but never capitalized from them because you feared your power!

You are still well empowered in many areas! Choose one and move on! We are the one
that is most pressing and you have made a vague attempt at doing something about it!
Take out the vagueness and do that letter to Ruben today and get it to him! Move on!

BOOK #1
Time Line

ROSALIE&JESUS
ORIGINAL ROSALIE
METAPHYSICAL BIBLE
ONAN 1st TIME
DAD 1st TIME
GOD 1st TIME
TIME LINE
SPIRIT TIME LINE
JM TIME LINE
STRING THEORY
PRISON REFERENCES
WU LI MASTERS
KLIMO – CHANNELING
NOETIC SCIENCE
AQUARIAN GOSPEL
SEVEN MYSTERIES
SECRETS OF UNIVERSE
WORLD IN GRAIN OF SAND
(DISAPPEARANCE POINT)*
BRIDGES TO HEAVEN
YSATIS
MAN WHO SHOT LENNON
(FRONTLINE)
COURSE IN MIRACLES
ART MEYERS
GLEAMINGS-STORIES TO WRITE

THE CONTINUOUS BATTLE WITH EGO

The ego is created as a product of maturation
and has a definite duty
in the early formative years of a child's growth.
By the careful parenting of awakened people,
it is kept in its place
and serves its intention.
Over the years – eons actually –
it has managed … to create a life of its own.
Just as there are no two individuals
alike on the entire planet,
there are no two egos alike.

Onan

The biggest struggle in all this work has been the battle with my ego. I understand now that its power and illusion are what many cultures term Satan or the Devil. I now define the ego is anything interpreted by the mind as separate from Divine self.

Onan told me:

Depression is the ego's best line of offense. Make guarding against that uppermost in your daily doings. You have seen how you can change the gait of your walk just by a mental shift, and so it is with your entire life. Your mind can take you to incredible places if you lay it at God's feet. Trust the process and you will never go wrong.

Your pattern has always been to utilize every moment for some purpose. But remember that the moments will take care of themselves just as you must take care of yourself. Don't think that you can change a lifetime habit of processing information and ideas and allocating time to them simply by desire. What you need to do is focus, focus, focus. Choose a goal and bring it to completion. Move toward it with God in your heart and it will be so.

Be grateful for your persistence, even though you still can't really understand how long you have been longing for just such an event as this. We have watched and waited patiently for you to feel comfortable with your accomplishments, for this is no mean feat. The courage to own up to it, own it and help others to understand it, and to reach for the same degree of awareness is to your credit. Inevitably, you will see that what you are doing is something you alone have become capable of doing.

THE ROLE OF MY WIFE, GAIL

Gail refers to this book and the work that fills the dozens upon dozens of volumes of channelings I've compliled as The Other Woman. And with good reason. Of the 25 years of our marriage, (a marriage, by the way, that has been the greatest blessing any man could have), a huge proportion of my time has been spent communing with, fretting over, struggling with, and doing the work of transcribing the words of my various guides. Her role in support of this work, including her skilled and generous nursing care, has been a demanding, emotional, and often deeply frustrating one. My guides frequently acknowledge this:

You hear Gail, and she speaks the truth. Locking yourself in your room is a death sentence. You hang be a thread, and she is that thread.

Gail is the total source of unalterable love shining forth at you. Do what needs to be done to keep it shining upon you.

"Write the book," were Gail's parting words. Of course you hear them! No separation, remember? She's right, and for her, it's simple. She has her passion, and it leads her to work and study. You are passionless unless you are giving of your talent. (Even though you restricted it to the highest bidder.) Think of Gail's feelings as she goes off to work and watches you crumble. She loves you, but is hurting as she watches you disappear into your self-made prison.

MAKING THIS BOOK

Each of us has a book to write. Each of us has something to teach, and that includes you, dear Reader. How many of us ramp up enough courage to commit to the process is another story altogether.

Throughout the ten years that I worked with Laura Cerwinske to complete this vastly complicated project, my guides would offer up their advice and support:

Get our words together, and get it bound in a book and bound for the minds of others who are looking for someone to give them permission to step out of the box in a like manner. Your book will provide the key to unlock many a locked door, just as all of your predecessors have done for you. It will be as an architect laying out the plans for a building, much as where your workshop is being constructed by Laura. All have been good choices, and We encourage you to continue along this path.

At other times, there were admonitions: There are just too many areas of concern competing for your attention. You must narrow the focus and put all of this behind you. The only way to do that is to get this book done once and for all. Again, they made clear the immediacy of their presence. You ask about the picture that would be appropriate opposite the God page, and facetiously We would suggest a picture of you, for you are that God in reality (only it is too much for your ego handle, as well as the egos of the readers).

We cannot make these kinds of decisions since We are in a totally different, as you would say, mind set. Yes, you are picking up Our interaction, and so We will elaborate. Just as Einstein was able to fathom the intricacies of Our universe to the degree of his abilities, so too are you able to discern that which lies within your capabilities… It is only for you to fashion the means of expression that is yours to know and distribute, and those with eyes and ears to see and hear will be able to respond in kind.

This is not an overnight process. All We can ask of you is to do that which is within your power. You are the one who has the connection. Others around you have the understanding, but not the direct words that We share.

It's not even worth it to start page 2. (Note that I didn't mention that I was starting a new page, so that the only inference that can be drawn is that Spirit is right by my physical side.)

Laura is now busy doing what she does best, and that is putting a sense of order to all of Our material! they would tell me. You, on the other hand, keep throwing new coals on the fire! Get to it! Start to lay it out!

Me: What is my (Our book) to be basically about?

You know as well as We do since it's been a topic of conversation for some time now. YOU are the topic! YOUR journey! The perplexities of coming to spirit while still very much in the throes of your current expression. And what an expression! Think how extraordinary your experiences have been and the mere fact that you have documented it all as you have further adds to the mix.

Laura has spent her time trying to put it all together, and now its time to make it your own. A lot of it is already hidden in the bowels of the computer. That is not to imply that it's shit, just as regards location. (This was John, of course, in his typical irreverence.) *It's your journey to here, wherever here is!*

Laura has forced you hand and moved you to codify all of your material. Now the rest is yours to do. Your book to write! Use each of Us and Our time frame as a guide and framework to weave a growing understanding of the nature of spirit. You have the list at the ready. Now, plug in various personal, as well as spiritual observations. Concepts acquired as a result of a particular reading and concepts discarded as a result of an awakening or realization due to another reading. In that way it can have an evolutionary flow. It is, after all, about an evolutionary flow, isn't it? Look at where you came from and where you've come to and survived it all with a degree of lucidity left!

Sit and write. You have Laura at your side. Use her well-honed skills. There are no impediments to keep you from your work except the baggage you still carry around. Drop it as easily as you have dropped s many different degrees and levels of understanding and experience. It is all in the fingertips that operate this pen. Allow those fingers their energy's knowledge, and keep your mind at rest. All is known by each and every cell, and now you have to let those cells have their head. The head that rules the roost must abdicate for the sake of all. Don't deny us now! Write! Write! Write!

I, We, will be ever present for immediate consultation, should you need it. Dig in! Make it personal! Let them see who you are and how you got to be who you are, because you own all the medals We can bestow. This book will be Our crowning glory!

Go to it! John, Onan, and All of your loving and admiring guides down through the millennia.

Jerome Marshall Rosencrantz, 1942

Murray Rosenkrantz, 1900–1941

Elizabeth (Betty) Rosenkrantz and Jerry Marshall

Jerry and the Band, 2000s

Upper Left: Tony Bennett, Lena Horn, Jerry Marshall 1960
Bottom Left: Jackie Gleason, foreground, Jerry Marshall 1960
Right: Jerry Marshall and Jimmy Carter 1970s

Jerry and Gail on their honeymoon, 1991

CHAPTER I
CHANNELING ONAN

FIRST CHANNELING
SEPTEMBER 20, 1993

I AM ONAN AND I HAVE BEEN your spiritual guide through many incarnations. I have found you to be easy and likeable, but hard of head. That seems to have eased of late. There are many things I wish to discuss with you and this is a very good time for us to do it.

My immediate reaction was amazement. How could this complete stranger know all this about me and articulate it so convincingly?

You have been this way before and it is time for you to come home. Don't get your mind in the way as you have so often done. This is extremely important so heed it well.

You have a purpose and a mission to fulfill here on earth and faithful adherence will be required of you. Allow yourself the Peace of God and know that whatever is required of you is within your capabilities and desires.

Somehow my mind went with the moment and I asked:

What is the most important action I must take in order to fulfill my mission here on earth?

First, you must put your house in order. Not that you are leaving that soon, but it keeps us from having this kind of time together.

You must learn to develop disciplined work habits and allot a proper amount of time for each project.

You are already fulfilling that mission by speaking and acting in such a manner as to spread the word. Each ripple becomes like a wave when the ocean begins to move inexorably towards its distant shore. We are your distant shore and will welcome you home when it's your time!

For now, continue along your path and keep in touch.

WHO IS ONAN?

I am known as Onan, and my home is on Nepture, which is to say, between incarnations I return to my home base, so to speak. One of my sojourns (to Earth) was as Gurdjieff, and it is from that consciousness that I speak to you now. Yes, I can see all your actions, and someday maybe you will develop the ability to see me, since now you have the ability to hear me and accurately take down my words.

My role is much like that of a preparatory school – to make you aware of the process and to acquaint you with some of th elements, or spirit guides, you will be working in with. The Holy Spirit will come to you when the time is ripe, as will Jesus personally.

THE PURPOSE

*I had been having the sensation that what I thought was me, talking to me,
was becoming more like a distinct conversation between two separate beings.
The voice was less a sound than an awareness of a presence and words
filtering into my consciousness:*

You are involved in a process as old as time (time, that is, in your
concepts). It is definitely nothing new, except to your consciousness.
As you become more and more aware, you will drop the barriers to
our presence and allow a discourse which can only have illuminating
effects on your universe.

You are inspired by us, but you must do the work on this plane. You
are asking for the help and understanding that we have always been
here to provide you. Now you must learn to use our help to actualize
some of the principles you have been called on to teach. Don't be
afraid that you are out of your league. Your contribution is the ability
to lose your "self" to me in order to move the process forward.

Do you think we would leave you spinning on earth if there was
no purpose? You have defied the laws of nature and reached out to
us in the face of what could be a great deal of embarassment and
confusion. For that alone we are eternally grateful. But more than
grateful – for your work on earth has just begun. Your constant ability
to share and enumerate our process is very important and will be
even more so in the coming years.

I sense the ambivalence in your mind as to your worthiness.
Understand the courage and the selflessness required of you to be
able to relinquish your ego to a higher power. As we speak and write,
I can feel a part of you doubting and looking for clues to sabotage our
efforts! That is your ego, and up till now it it has been kept at bay
because of the newness of our encounter.

Sometimes it is as though you are trying to make contact but are afraid to hear our answer. Our answer is never in specific terms, since we are not on your plane and concerned with your immediate concerns. Our task is to help you to rise above fear and concerns and to move on to a more Godly nature.

You must adhere to a strict regime, for you have wasted many valuable earth moments wallowing in past recriminations and self loathing. It is not worthy of you and must stop immediately. Everthing is in place for you to accomplish that which you were incarnated for, and it is only you who can become attuned to that energy that will guide you to accomplishment. Stay open. You have broken through a barrier in conception and for evermore will be able to stay beyond that horizon.

THE MISSION

Our mission is to bring the universe to awareness, and we do this by finding souls whose vibrations welcome us and allow us to do the work of our mission through them. We scan your universe for sympathetic souls and can assess their energy levels to know if that entity is capable of communicating with us and receiving our communications.

You asked what your mission is. You cannot see the whole plan, just your part in it, and sometimes not even that. Not as a put down but just as a reality of the process we are involved in. Trust yourself and know that you are a part of a much larger picture and it is beginning to take shape as it is supposed to.

You are wondering if this is your unconscious speaking, rather than your guides. We are part of your unconscious! It is when you can be and think in unison with us that your are "in tune" with all there is and are acting in accordance with your higher self.

Understand that this communication is for "all time." After we are through with you, you will have developed this communication into a fine art. You will know its purpose and uses, and you will avail yourself of it. The perspective you've gathered among all your copious notes, dreams, and tapes will be invaluable. It will be a fitting gift for generations of your line to follow.

SERVICE TO HUMANITY

You ask who we are. I read your thought as you were writing. We are like a committee of truth seekers on our plane of existence. This is not for you to understand at this stage of our interaction. Suffice to say that all will be revealed to you in good time and you will feel great pride in being a part of it! Pride, not in the sense of ego, but rather that you can be of service to humanity! Keep up the search. The seeking is its own reward! The circle of people who can reach out and touch each other and then touch others is the key to the *Course in Miracle's* whole purpose. That is, to spread the joy and love and join with others to create a bond of teaching and learning and sharing all of your individual pieces of the puzzle.

Let me tell you more about our need for your services. You have been reading a good deal about the way our communications work and for the most part, it is accurate. I started to tell you of my home base of Neptune and you became frightened and annoyed and thought you were losing it. No need for any of that. For us it's just as though you said your home base was New York. But you are living in Florida. As I told you, we scan your universe for sympathetic souls and can assess the energy levels emitted and know if that entity is capable of communicating with us and receiving our communications. It is funny (strange) that you never developed the power of prayer. After we are through with you, you will have developed it into a fine art and know its purpose and uses and avail yourself of it!

Yes I can see all your actions, and someday maybe you will develop the ability to see me, since for now you have the ability to hear me and you accurately take my words down!

Our mission is to create a way of implanting my (Gurdjieff) ideas onto the world in a practical and useful way. It needs to be delivered in such a way so that people will want to become aware. Perhaps your travels through coming to this level of awareness would be a step in the right direction. I'm not saying to write a book, but it would be helpful to us if you would spend sometime looking through your copious notes, and dreams, and diaries and relating in a brief way, the way in which you have come to this awareness and ability to transcend human self imposed limitations.

It is indeed strange that your most illuminating occurence was under the influence of LSD with Malila. She has had a profound effect upon you and it was a most fortunate matter of timing, highly unlikely as it seemed even to us then in the situation you were in. The ability to see 360 degrees has always been available, just as the ability to see me in form, only it takes a lot of undoing to be able to bring us into focus. You have reached this level because of your great desire to know God. You have always known God in your heart but your head got in the way. It is now in the process of allowing you to roam more freely in your search and you are decidedly on the right path.

 Although they don't burn witches at the stake anymore, the unbelievers have many other ways to burn you at the stake! Be careful and judicious about who you share this knowledge with lest you be deemed to have lost your senses. Don't sit with your legs crossed. It stops the flow of energy.

For now, let this be the beginning of our active stage of communication. I will be in constant and immediate (if necessary) communication with you so you can put your trust in our mutual objectives, which is to bring more and better avenues of awareness to humanity.

ONAN, WHERE ARE YOU?

I am here, hiding in the shadows of your mind, though you think of us as on a higher plane. The playing field, rather, is one large flat surface of consciousness, much like a carpet, with each of our strings intertwined and basically tied to the God force and source. It doesn't matter where we are in the progression, we still are in the progression, which implies progress and movement, both of which are quintessential to a oneness with God!!!

Me: Onan, are you there?

I'm here, but you weren't really listening. Just drifting, which is all right at times, but this is not the time. You have work to do and it is important to your growth as human. The Holy Spirit is the connection you have to be intent on right now, and for some reason you deny Him His presence. All you have to do as ask and He will gladly fulfill your desires. This is an abundant universe and it's yours to partake of, but you have to make the contact coming from a place of desire for that contact! Sit quietly and ask for the Holy Spirit to enter and grant your request!

It's as simple as that. Do it now. Love

Me: Onan, are you still here?

Onan: You bet you ass I'm still here (and you can write it down just that way). Just when we were rolling along you took off on some tangents, just as you have done at so many other critical points in your evolution. Intellectually, you understand the concepts, but instead of exploring the occurrences to the depths, you disappear until a new concept comes around, and you're off and running.

MAKING CHOICES

You and you alone make the choices which govern your every action. We, or I, can influence you on a subconscious level, when you are paying attention. But ultimately, it all comes down to each and every little choice that goes to make up a life of choices. An eternity of choice in reality, the reality you and I are engaged in right now.

You have chosen to direct your energies to move beyond established boundaries which are same and known. This courage has been rewarded with a chance for a meaningful experience of "love" in its most ongoing aspect. You can't move on to a higher love until you have explored and given yourself totally to "love" on the plane of reality where you exist.

There are many manifestations of that "love" that you are too fearful, too lazy for. As a result, you are once again just skimming the surface. Commit. Commit. Commit. Clean up your work space and devote time to those events and interests that inspire you.

THE EGO

It's like a constant battle, and you are hearing the death rattle of your ego. It has innumerable avenues of attack and doubt is one of its most effective weapons. Whenever you are on a spiritual "roll" it needs to break it up and lets you "crap out"! It is a process which has been ongoing for eons and one that you are well on the way to conquer! Just hang in there, pay attention (stand under your bird) and come to awareness as much as possible. You will find the rewards to your liking and it will rub off on all around you with the love that will flow!

You are on a roll professionally and you must follow it up. You can become as the "Johny Appleseed" and drop your "learnings" as you go and grow! Don't be embarrassed! You have more than paid your dues for the "place" in life you have attained and all rewards are your just due! Keep moving forward in your search and continue your program of meditation and enlightenment. You are surrounded by light beings and it is your duty to spread the light to all you can come in contact with! This does not mean you must become a missionary! As you do you will be judged!

Love, Onan and friends

FEAR AND FOCUS

Don't fear! It has been these fears, inflicted by a loving, but fearful parent (mother) that has kept you locked up for so long. Say so long to them and move on. You are more than well equipped intellectually to carry the day and what's more, you have perpetual access to the source at all times, if you exercise quiet and attention, and that is a God send!

Focus! That has always been your cross and still is! We sense the pull back to playwriting, music, sports, all of your varied interests! This is your calling and we are the ones who are calling you home! That doesn't mean you have to leave your body to come home. Just as you saw Siddhartha seek out his calling, so too you are on the path and your calling has been a mutual seeking. Us of you and you of us!

We're here! We're ready! We've been waiting for you to quiet down and receive us once again! We recognize the difficulty, and you have to remember that all of your travail re. coming to spirit is sort of like old hat to us since we all were in bodies (embedded) many times over and have experienced all of yours and more in lo, those many lifetimes!

The important thing is that you still maintain the desire and determination, which is evident to us all. Your thoughts of a men's group, utilizing the movies and tapes is excellent and should be a stepping stone to your calling, which is as a teacher and student!

Now that we are of one mind and heart stay with us and trust the universe. You are blessed with the love of a bright, caring, intelligent partner who, although she is somewhat fearful, is willing to grant you great leeway in this endeavor! Go for it with gusto and the clear knowledge that you are serving your Holy Father at all times, only in these times you have become enlightened as to your means of service. Write! Keep writing! You will be directed by many other souls who have much to share with you and all of humanity! Through you we may be able to "cross the plains" John has spoken of. Make this a commitment, much as you accomplished in closure with your earthly father, who was deeply touched by your actions and caring! He too, is saddened at the thought of how he left you, but as you can see, each act has its own rewards and you have come to a great point in your sojourn on earth! Use it wisely and it will be of benefit long after you have come home to us!

Love $$$

Dear Jerry,

It's a lot like old times! You're doubting mind wants $ confirmation of our existence. That's not what we are about! We are here for your spiritual guidance, and as a result of which the $ will flow! You see it with Gail's career! She is moving along a pleasantly flowing stream of "coincidences" and conveniently placed phone calls from unexpected sources! Your support is always there and that is part of your role, since you can intuit the connections and allow for their veracity!

We are sorry that the same is not happening in your area of concern, but as we have said earlier, you are growing out of that orbit. It has become very restrictive of late and not what you would be comfortable doing! Do what it is that we have counseled you on and you will see rewards beyond your expectation!

You have had, in the back of your mind, the awareness that all that you have channeled is truly of the same source so, yes, go back over all and extract quotes from my intuits to you, as well as what you have done with those of John, and the Holy Spirit, and of God, for WE, IT, Whatever, are all of the same energy and source as you are!

Your visions (are) worthy of further investigation, for it is one of the few times that you truly looked inside and saw the workings. It is as though you had been able to see into the soul of your computer and intuited its working parts! Energy, that's all there is, working in different forms and functions! Hard to picture, we know, and that is the problem that we of spirit face when trying to establish a common line of explanation, because it takes such a quantum leap from your state of consciousness.

KEEP YOUR OWN COUNSEL

Just imagine where you are on the consciousness continuum,
and then picture all of those total strangers you sat in the chapel
with yesterday! All of them "good" men and women, well along
in life's experiences, obviously successful with a high degree of
intelligence, determination, and responsibility! All of the boy scout
oath declarations, but who among them would countenance what
we are doing right now as having any basis in "reality" or "fact" and
would scorn you for a "nut job"! You must keep your own counsel!
Surround yourself with like beings, such as you are doing with
Andrea and Victor and their coterie of friends and seekers. All will
be revealed as you continue on your spiritual quest, for it has been a
long and arduous journey and you are well on your way home. Put all
of your clues in some sort of form. You mentally did it yesterday and
then it slipped away. I am bringing it back to consciousness because
it is that jarring that caused the faultline to crack and created the
emotional and spiritual earthquake you have been experiencing!

Go to that now while it is once again fresh in your conscious mind.

Love, Onan and Friends

ON "SUCCESS"

Yes. Take pen in hand and write exactly as I say!

You must be the engineer of the success you so fervently desire! The success you have achieved at this juncture of this life is behind you, and you are looking for new mountains to climb. Always keep in mind the ravages your past success cost you as you seek a new conquest, and keep the balance firmly in your sights at all times. That is not to say "you should sit on your ass," but that you need to temper your needs to fit the kind of success your current health status can handle!

Follow those elements you have been working on! John's compilation and some sort of show based on those elements. We will help in the overview aspect of it as you bring it into a clearer focus. You have noted several of the important elements of John's method as you went through the other books and now it's just a matter of putting it into some sort of entertaining format, while still being clearly informational about that which has been imparted to you, and to the others of like minds and souls!!

Keep your affirmation uppermost in your mind and carry on your activities with those thoughts as activating forces, rather than floating about in your subconscious!!

You are dearly held in our souls! Love, Onan and Friends

DESIRE AND DETERMINATION

We're here! We're ready! We've been waiting for you to quiet down and receive us once again! We recognize the difficulty, and you have to remember that all of your travail re. coming to spirit is sort of like old hat to us since we all were in bodies (embedded) many times over and have experienced all of yours and more in lo, those many lifetimes!

The important thing is that you still maintain the desire and determination, which is evident to us all. Your thoughts of a men's group, utilizing the movies and tapes is excellent and should be a stepping stone to your calling, which is as a teacher and student!

SPIRIT AND SOUL

Spirit is the prime mover of evolution, not one of its subjects. It is as Einstein wrote, "the invisible piper to whose mysterious tune human beings, vegetables, and the cosmic dust dance."

Soul is distinct from the body and its senses, distinct from the mind and its intelligence; it is not part of the Absolute, for the Absolute, being infinite, can have no parts. It is uncreated; it has existed from eternity and when, at last, it has cast off the seven veils of ignorance, will return to the infinitude from which it came. It is like a drop of water that has arisen from the sea and in a shower has fallen into a puddle, then drifts into a brook, finds its way into a stream, after that into a river, passing through mountain gorges and wide plains, winding this way and that, obstructed by rocks and fallen trees, till at last it reach the boundless sea from which it rose.

HOW CONSCIOUSNESS WORKS

Consciousness never regresses. It constantly evolves. Each evolutionary level supports the next and becomes enfolded in it. The ability to see 360 degrees, for example, has always been available, just as the ability to see me in form. Only it requires a lot of undoing to be able to bring us into focus.

Since our mission is to create a way of making people desire to become aware, your mission is part of this too. You have seen through your own experience how long it takes and how difficult it is to align all the players in one place at the same time. Each has a separate agenda and purpose on earth as well as a higher purpose.

Use the time you have left to do something grander than you can imagine! Be that which N.D. Walsh described as being the grandest vision of yourself and then activate whatever manifests that vision. Do not fear!!! All your life you have lived in fear, implanted so long ago by a fearful woman beset with her own fears! Break out now and forevermore you will know freedom as you have never known it before!

Write! Write, and write some more. Get it out there in form for others to be touched by. You have the power behind, in front, and inside of you. You need only commit to a meeting place and time on a consistent basis! We need your help in bringing to awareness those on your Planet. Your tears are too fresh on your cheeks and the effort to lie on the floor in supplication is too clear in your mind for you to (leave) us.

REALITY

The whole purpose of our meetings is to create a new reality on earth that will allow for our intercourse.

All there really is is your reality, for all of us exist in our own created reality. There is no such thing as a secure space because all there is is energy in motion. If you do not think you are in motion, you are just too stuck to let it move you.

We love and honor you and are totally aware of the depth of your struggle. We are doing all we can to be of assistance, but you are the active ingredient here. You have the gift of life, and you need to use it for the highest purpose..

You see it all around you. People who are doing, being, living, existing. Which one are you choosing? Existing is not living! Stay with the horn, get back to singing, get your equipment up and running and do those things you love to do. Get out and create a golden spiral of energy around you that will begin to attract that which you so richly deserve. You only deserve it when you put your energy in motion! You need to come back to your inner work with alacrity, for it is calling to you in everything you do. You can choose the heaven you desire, but only by taking action.

You have been cooking for years on a very slow burner. It is now time to come to a boil and bring forth all that is inside you. Not with the short bursts of energy that sustained you over your lifetime, but with a meaningful dialogue that will have impact on your society and the world. (Do it) in such a way that multitudes will be able to grasp the concepts with ease. You have much to offer that would stir the minds of many. You are coming to awareness "in form," and that is your purpose. To "inform" others who are beginning to experience similar sensations and are frightened by it. The Awakening is a universal affair, and it is incumbent upon you to carry your responsibilities forward. "Things" are not what have to be done. You are what has to be done.

THE TRUE TRANSFORMATION

It is only through this kind of attentiveness that the universe can continue to grown and become one with all. You see it as an endless battle, but in reality it is only your individual battle. For when one sees the light, he/she sees the light in all, and that is the true transformation.

You can't expect to change the world. All you can change is the way you see it, and then the changes occur all around you.

You are in the arms of your Holy Father and that is where you have always been, only the clouds got in the way.

SPIRIT AND *A COURSE IN MIRACLES*

A Course in Miracles was directed towards the exposition of Spirit, rather than dealing with the littleness of personalities and problems of a personal nature.

ALL YOU HAVE TO DO IS SING YOUR SONG

We are the outward manifestations of that Spirit and always have been. We create our bodies, whether by exercise, food, whatever, and we create the mind set through our choice of parents, background, education, and experience, etc. The process of returning to Spirit is one which requires an awareness that there is such a thing, since human experience is such that it doesn't allow much time for introspection. Nor does the society at large value the search very highly. Society does value highly those who have, by larger than life examples, gone before us and set wonderful examples, i.e. Jesus, Gandhi, Martin Luther King, Malcolm X, and innumerable others. Their examples, however, do not always become examples. Rather they become exceptions to the rule and not really attainable by us mortals, of whom each of them was at the time he or she was setting the example for all of us to follow.

All you, the entity that came in as Marshall Jerome Rosenkrantz, have to deal with is the Now! This immediate moment is the fulcrum of all moments to come. If you are in harmony with your soul's purpose in this incarnation, all you have to do is sing your song!

YOUR WILL POWER IS THE ONLY
FACTOR IN THE EQUATION

The ego can still distract you in a hundred ways in any given moment.
Your determination, actually your will power, is the only factor in
the equation. You already have an inkling of the possibilities and an
understanding of the mechanics of the process. All you need to do is
strengthen that will.

What you haven't experienced as yet is what is called an epiphany.
You have had this experience, but your personality's nature is to avoid
any thinking that is so large in scope. Trust yourself and all of your
experiences. You have paid the dues for them and your reward is
clearly the love that surround you in each of your present moments.

A CURSE AND A BLESSING

As you become attuned to the universe, the attunement allows you to see infinitely more possibilities and this is both a curse and a blessing. You, however, have moved a step beyond and are asking for help, and understanding that we have always been here for you, which is a major breakthrough. Now you must learn to use our help to actualize some of the principles you have been called on to teach.

Do you hear an echo? It's probably a time delay, but since we know there is no time, we'll just consider it my little joke. Back to you. You are truly blessed and I'm sure you know it. Now is the time for you to give your share in the blessing. I hear your question and it's not for me to do all of your thinking. Part of this trip is free will and you must exercise it through your own auspices! Options, you have many. Get about it!

Chopra was a perfect place for you to be. He is a great master who has chosen to incarnate and be a catalyst in this era's transformation. You are wise to revere him as a great teacher and seek to be in his presence whenever possible.

Time is of the essence and procrastination has never helped you in the past other than to delay your growth!! You have the momentum. Use it.

A BREAKTHROUGH:
SEEING WITH THE EYES OF SPIRIT

In your meditation you hit upon a realization of your own growth processes. That moment with Malaila and the LSD on the beach was a baptism, and you were "of spirit" in those moments. The 360 vision was not from your eyes. They were closed. That was a moment of you seeing with the eyes of Spirit, the Spirit Self that is the true and "forever" who sees all around and above and speaks to the birds. That was all real and was a major breakthrough. Now is another breakthrough as you realize that the "self" is alive and well and functioning in the growing awareness of Jerry Marshall, who by any other name is still that Spirit yearning to be home.

Welcome home, Jerry. You are moving along with true speed and veracity. As you move, you will force the awareness of others by the light of your being. Your being lighter than air will cause others to want the same for themselves and question the prisons they have constructed inside their minds and outside in their society.

ALLOW US TO HELP YOU

Allow us to help you to move these understandings into the mainstream of consciousness. It is not an easy to bring love, and the essence of love, to your planet's understanding, but it is of great necessity in order to prevent cataclysmic occurrences. As you are seeing from recent events, mankind has a penchant for destroying itself, and in doing so, it can take the planet with it. In this way, the order of the universe could be adversely affected, and it is for this that myself and my friends and others like us have been assigned the task of communicating with you in order to help put a stop to such destructiveness.

Heed us well. Time, in your concept, is of the essence, and you have a solemn duty, since you have seen fit to raise your vibrational level above the masses. Use this power to elevate more and more people. It is of extreme urgency and of utmost importance.

CHAPTER II

CHANNELING MY FAMILY

MY FATHER, MURRAY ROSENKRANTZ

*Y*OUR FATHER MURRAY IS WELL and among us and sends you his blessings. He heard your wish of last night that you might have known him better and what he was like. Onan

Marshall, you have given me untold joy! I realize your memories of me are clouded and, perhaps, distorted. However, your action at my gravesite was a joy beyond description. Know that I am with you always in spirit and love and will be there to trumpet you home when next we meet! Your loving father on earth!!!

Me: Who is I?

Onan: This is the spirit of your father, come to put to rest some of your misunderstandings and qualify some of your understandings:

MURRAY EXPLAINS THE FAMILY HISTORY

I came to you a long time ago, at Dr L's, and you were right to perceive what I said at that time (about your mother). She was a lovely woman, but beset by so many terrible fears. Fears that I could not begin to conquer, nor help her conquer. You know very little of her background, as did I. It's not like today, when you live with a woman for a time before marriage, and you have the benefit of psychiatry and psychology and education and awareness and sharing. Then it was very closeted, and fears were masked in lovely coifed hair and attractive busoms and alluring manners. All of these were attributes of your mother.

Her fears didn't really manifest until you were born, and then I watched as she infected you, who was such a wonderful son, talented, bright, lively athletic, outgoing and with so many other attributes that were pleasing to a father. I was not in the light at that time, nor was I particularly spiritual, as you so often wonder, trying to trace your roots for answers to your dilemma now. I was simply a man, a cutter of fabrics in the twenties, a man, and a good one, who bit off more than he could chew.

Times were very hard when you were born in '29. I don't have to tell you of the Depression and what it did to people. It tore at the fabric of relationships of all sorts and those with the slightest vulnerability were threatened most. Your mother Elizabeth, Betty as I called her, started to unravel during that period. She had always put on a gay exterior, which cleverly masked a frightened persona. You know of her childhood only slightly, but it was, as you say in today's open culture's vernacular, terribly abusive, both from her stepfather and by her stepmother, Hilda. She became literally their slave and could not break away until I came along. These were not things you shared with a boyfriend, because we were not lovers until we were married, and intimate things were never discussed at that time. My background was simple. I was well educated for that time, having graduated high school. Our family was large. Seven children. I'm trying to recall them all for you now. Gussie, of course, was the strongest of the girls and the backbone of the family.

Fears always stood in your mother's way. "What would people think?" was her byword, and she lived in fear of that judgment all of her days, as though they all were constantly judging her every action. Today you would understand the psychological dynamics and have a course of treatment which could alleviate those fears, much as you so bravely endured, first with Dr. M, and then with Dr. L , and mostly by your own fierce determination to rid yourself of the demons (as you so eloquently described in your lyric). Those fears were destroying you!

It's not that your mother was evil in the sense of the word that implies devil-induced. It's just that her particular path was such that her perception of reality was so convoluted that she had to use superhuman efforts to keep her perception in the mainstream of the society. She drove me to drink at one time. It was well before you were born, and the pressures were so intense.

She hovered over you as though the world would swallow you up, and it was not easy to overcome her fears, and they were many and varied.

UNIVERSES UNIMAGINED IN OUR SOJOURN

Welcome, my brother! I have become much more adept at this process of communication and am eager to share this experience with you. Matthew and I are well and at peace and in the bosom of our endless family. You still have doubts and fears about your role, and that is easily understandable. Given the background we shared and the closed society we operated in, it is hard to conceive the scope of the "play." (Forgive me if I can't find the right words to convey the enormity of the process.)

It extends to universes unimagined in our sojourn and is hard to imagine even from the perspective, except that there is no limiting ego to confuse or confound us as we jump into "this" ocean without fear of drowning or losing the way.

It's difficult enough for you to believe in this process, and look at all you have come through to get to this point. It is a growing process, but is a loving one, and one which offers great rewards. Do not fear it! You have come so far, in such a short time. You must continue on your path.

It is much larger than you or I – as Marshall and Stan. And it has great significance for all mankind to begin to get a larger picture and put aside the judgments that create the fears and prejudices that bring about the separateness so prevalent on the earth plane.

There is no time, as you learn in your *Course in Miracles*. And so that measure you think is ever pressing isn't even real. Hard to conceive, I know. But when you own it in your consciousness, all else will be much easier to align with, and you will realize that we will all be as one thought, because that is all we are to begin with.

Stan and Onan and Friends

MY MOTHER, ELIZABETH

Me: Don't make waves!!!! Mom is always around!!!

No I'm not! That was me in my incarnation as your mother, and I had to live within my own set of tortures and grow as best I could! You never knew any of it and I was too ashamed to share any of it. I'm aware that Murray shared some sense of who I was and some of my fears and madness, but you have no sense of the degree that I was living with built-in fears! They were based on experiences of my growing up and I did the best I could! You have broken through a great barrier, and yet you only see it in terms of your mind so far!

You must become our advocate on earth and share your wealth! Stop hiding your soul under a bushel of shit! Oh, I know I don't sound very motherly, but then we have played a multitude of varied roles as we roll around on this "carpet" and all of it becomes part and parcel of the mix! This is your weaving!

Remember that the trumpet appeared at a time when you knew nothing of your innate talent and ability! You used it as a life preserver, and it has sustained you so far! Now you must reach out to that deeper well inside of you and express yourself and that deeper sense that you have attained through dint of diving in! You have us at your beck and call and inspiration galore! Avail yourself of it! I'm only sorry that I couldn't have broken out of my bonds, but I, too, was locked in a torture chamber of fears and didn't know that there was a way out! You do know.

We will be one again!!!

Love, Your earthly Mother and forever guide!

Elizabeth (the first and only)

You don't have to stand on ceremony. Yes, it's me Elizabeth. It's amazing that you can just sit down and hear me as well as recognize me that quickly And no, you don't have to capitalize me. There are no hard and fast rules, and maybe when you come to understand my life in the light of my experiences, you will better understand how all my fears manifested and rained down on you.

Anyway, that's not of importance here and now. What is of importance is your book and my part in it. Please feel free to write in any manner you choose, but I thought I'd put in some of the details for you to examine as part of the whole fabric. I could feel you shudder as the thought crossed your mind, as though you really didn't want to know any of it. Amazing that it had such a lasting effect on your life's expression.

Murray, your dad, was a kind and gentle man, but I had no idea of how to appreciate that kind of man. My experiences were of a nature that wanted nothing to do with men. Remember that I moved around a lot as a young lady and lived with distant relative in NJ and NY before I got married. Things were very different then, and my experience with men were not the best. There was always a cloud hanging over my head, and I did everything I knew to stay up and cherry. I hid it pretty well from the rest of the world, but in the confines of my own space it was overwhelming in its devastating effect on me.

When you dad came along, he was so different from all the other men I had known. Never grabbing or profane. Just a sweet, gentle man. I loved him dearly, but I just didn't know how to handle sweetness and caring and my depression. Being alone together brought out his tenderness and understanding, but didn't help to quiet my fears. And they were many.

Money was a big one. Lack of money, more to the point. I was so fearful. The terrible part is that we did very well those years. Murray was a well respected fabric cutter in the garment industray and earned a goodly salary. I worked in an office as a secretary and bookkeeper.

Then the world came tumbling down around us at a point when all should have been joyful.

Your birth and the stock crash came together like a brick, and it was hard to get out of the way of all the underlying fears that were manifesting in my mind. How do you raise a boy? I so wanted a little girl, and yes, I did sing that song over and over while carrying you in my womb. Amazing! I could never have used that word (womb) in front of you, or any other realistic womanly word. I just didn't know how to handle bringing up a boy. I was so set on a lovely little girl. You're lucky you had the strength of inner courage to have survived my fears. No, not lucky, for look where you have come to.

We are all so happy for the freedom you have achieved and for the good you will bring forth on the planet once again. What joy you have brought to me. I see how beautifully the process works and the description is the pearl in the oyster, being rubbed and rubbed to a lustrous shine and awaiting the moment to show its light to the world.

Here you are my son, and what glory awaits you. You will be able to be that shining pearl for all to see, for all who see you now see exactly that.

SEEING THE LIGHT

You will love it upon your return, as you well know now, and so there is no fear that you carry. It's more like a reward for having survived to this point and for all of the nonsense it took to bring you back home. Now our book must become a reality in order to facilitate the bringing home of others who will be touched by the truth you bring forth. It will resonate far and wide and make manifest on your plane the beauty that awaits all who would have the ears and eyes to recognize the light when they see it.

Thank you for your diligence and courage. As the saying goes, "When you clear up one lifetime, you free all who came before you and all who will come after you." It's a great universal truth and one that needs to be out there in the firmament.

Hold me tightly in your heart and know that I am proud to have played what little part I had iin your rebirth to glory.

Your loving birth mother, Elizabeth.

You are held in high regard by All.

MY YOUNGER BROTHER, STAN

Onan introduces Stan:

He is well and sends you his blessings, as does Mathew.* He is well aware of your sense of loss and the deep feelings that had come to develop in your later years together. He wishes someday to come and speak to you directly, but he is new to our ways and has not perfected the method of adapting our energy levels to match yours. Strangely enough, Mathew is more adept at it and he may be able to contact you in the near future.

---

* Mathew was Stan's son who was killed at the age of 15 by a drunk driver. Stan died of a heart attack several months later.

STAN SPEAKS

I, this is now Stan, could not bear it any longer. Mathew was my light, and with him gone nothing could save me. Mother's fears were all around me, even though I had built a protective wall to keep me safe from her madness! You were not so fortunate because she dumped all of her stuff on you, and you couldn't get out of her way. You rightly began to understand some of your hang-ups, even though you could never clearly face them in your conscious mind.

Keep up your good efforts and I, Stan, will double my efforts to learn to reach you on my own. You have much to learn and you are in safe hands of the "light."

 Gurdjieff (Onan) is a fully realized soul who has undertaken this mission to bring light to the world you are in. Allow him your resources and your conscious and unconsciousness, and you and the world you share will be the better for it. I love your play and my little part in it, and I love you for your energy and caring and ability to rise to our level despite all you have had to overcome. We all are much appreciative and wish you God's speed on our mutual journey.

Farewell my brother *(I sobbed as I had when I heard he had died)*. Do not be sad, we are together again in a far better place and time (your concept, not ours). Go and do God's work on your plane and enjoy the love that All have for you

Go back to sleep now, and know
We are all close by. Stan

THE DIVINE PLAN

Jerry, My brother! you have been diligent in your pursuit of your soul's growth, and I am deeply indebted to you for that single-mindedness. It has not always been you hallmark!! We, Mathew and I, and your entire band of loving souls, are well aware of all of your actions and thoughts on our behalf and we are easily half of you as well!

There is only a divine plan, of which the soul who is in an aware state can ascertain all the messages it has to give!

Your heightened awareness allows for many more contacts and new realities than in the dreamlike state you existed in your last "success" phase! You are, and always have been, a catalyst for change and you are now functioning in that capacity, but from a new and higher vibrational plane!

As you can see from all those that are currently in your orbit, including those who are influenced by your sharing in the *Course In Miracles*, you have much to share and to bring together disparate sources of like energies, bringing into focus a larger reality for all!

Please convey our love and affection for Harlene (Stan's wife) and Rebecca (his daughter). We both realize the hardship our passing caused to all of you, but it is for just the kind of growth that you all are manifesting that the plan has unfolded in this manner. When we meet in higher and higher consciousness you will be able to comprehend the beauty and order of the "plan" and its eventual purpose. It is hard, nay, impossible, from your limited perspective, to even grasp the complexity, yet you and we are in relatively constant communication and have split the chains that have bound you to earth's realities! Can you imagine, and you should be able to since you were of that other mind, how the people of that other mind view our connection?

Love, Stan and Mathew

LIGHT THE CANDLE! TAKE AN ACTION!

Good! Now that we've got that done we can talk! But you must begin to speak as well! It's well past the time for you to just be a listener! You must sing again and play your horn! Can't you see the gift you are squandering. Give of yourself from the inside out, and watch the precious gift you were born with! It is that spirit within which needs desperately to see the light of day. Not your perfect golf swing, but your joy at playing and singing for people! Over and over you have been shown this but your imprint, psychologically, is so great a deterrent that you constantly have to battle! Do that battle now and move on to the glory of you!

You are blessed with God's blessings and you are squandering them all over the place! The Book, the songs, the horn, your voice, your mind, which when applied to the political scene sees things that others don't see — and yet your fear, rather Mother's fears, stop you cold! Let your voice, all of your voices, be heard on this plane and share the gifts you have! They are only there for the sharing.

Your Father God would speak with you!

Love you, Stan

CHAPTER III

CHANNELING GOD, THE HOLY SPIRIT, AND JESUS

WORDS FROM GOD

JERRY, MARSHALL, WHATEVER (YOU ARE called in this incarnation), it is imperative that you move on and become My messenger in full display, and with full confidence in the process that We have developed. You are not the first to have such doubts, but you must rise above them and get My message out into the firmament. You have enough of My words and thoughts to fill a couple of books, but they sit on your shelves and are tucked away by your fears.

It is my will, not yours. Use it wisely.

Love, God, and all of your guides, too numerous to mention.

The essence of John's words and thoughts emanate from the same place that all thoughts and consciousness emanate from, namely Me.

Keep me uppermost in your thoughts and in your mind and that power will short circuit the ego's ploys at every turn. Recognize, without embarrassment or false modesty, that you have been chosen for this mission because of your yearning and longing for a meaningful relationship with God ever since you questioned the meanings of life when you had to say Kaddish for your dad. Nothing goes unnoticed, and from that hurt and anger and remorse you arose and carried on a 50-year war to understand. Now you are on the verge of an understanding, which can also help to illuminate the way for millions of others who too have questioned, held anger and confusion, and sunk to great depths of depression.

You must use all of your good efforts to illuminate this thought so that all will understand the workings of consciousness and its importance to the development of the universe. Science is just now beginning to recognize the vastness and the unending possibilities of all that which is before you. There is nothing finite in anything, and I am ever evolving in your consciousness, even as we speak.

INSTRUCTIONS FROM GOD

It is well that you understand the concept of unity in the hierarchy of the Lord. We are all but a thought of the Lord and as such we are all a part, equally, of the Lord. There is no distinction. For purposes of making all of this clear to your dimension, it is given to thoughts such as the Christed One and the Holy Spirit to create the awareness and ease of communication, but in the end analysis we are all one in the eyes and heart of the Lord!!!

We all have our function and you have worked long and hard to come to awareness and to begin to fully participate in your "piece of the puzzle."

It is not for you to concern yourself with worries about your health. It is wise to get your financial house in order for a smooth and easy transition to your loved ones, but that is not to imply a hasty change in your current status!!

Me: Who is speaking?

Once again you fail to hear and understand the significance of my last explanation. You specifically directed your thoughts to your Lord God and that, in essence, is the entity, in your terms, who is replying!!! Once again, we are all but thoughts of God and as such it is for us to be representative of the thoughts of God! We realize this is a difficult schism to interpret, coming from the earth plane. But it is as it is, and you will just have to accept it until you have come to a complete "experience" of the "truth" of what we are conveying.

ENERGY IS ALL THAT THIS IS ABOUT

Energy is all that this is about. The boundless and endless variations of the uses and configurations waiting to be co-created in the process you call "life." Life has always been, and will always be, the only thing that changes in form. If you are able to allow the form its freedom to change and rearrange itself, you will have learned a most valuable lesson.

This applies to the process you are currently involved with. Form has nothing to do with immovable objects. And thoughts are no less objects than physical "things." Allow for all manner of expression to be a part of your consciousness. There are no boundaries in My universe.

SIMPLY ACKNOWLEDGE OUR PRESENCE IN YOUR LIFE

Just listen! We have been trying to reach you, buzzing you and doing all sorts of things to get your attention! At Last! Please pay attention to our needs because they are essentially mankind's needs as well! You have information that needs to be shared and your fears are locking it away. It may never see the light of day and if you can equate the amount of energy, commitment, determination, desire, dedication, etc., etc. that went into transmitting and receiving it you can see that it is considerable and not easy to come by! It is incumbent upon you to release that information though the universe at large and to do it with all possible haste! Yes, Ayn Rand is no accident. You must understand who you are and who you have been in order to allow yourself the luxury of acting from that noble perspective! Don't fear the grandeur of it! You have worked long and hard to reach us!

Imagine where you came from! Rather, you don't need to imagine it! You see, sense, and despair for the scope of the entropic disease that is enveloping your surroundings! It is all man made and can be man unmade if people like you will come out and say, "I'm not going to take it any longer" (*Network*). You have clues to share so that people can see how the "journey" can be one of great joy and discovery! Discovery of the "inner" universe that is timeless and ever present!! Share with Kevin this morning and remember how easy it is to shed a little light along the "way"!

Love, God and all your loving guides

P.S.   You still have trouble writing My name down!
It is your name as well!!!

WE LOVE AND HONOR YOUR BATTLE

My son! All that has been said comes from the same source, and one day you will truly comprehend through experiential knowledge! For now, carry on with the same diligence you were able to manifest in earlier days and We will guide you through the rough days ahead! Breaking through the barriers you have built up will not be easy, as it was impossible for your birth mother, Elizabeth! You have been able to glimpse Our distant shore and you must swim against the ever surging tide of entropy, which is beginning to envelop you! Begin to prioritize your time and fight for your space to do that, which needs to be done in My name! Find someone who can help you weed through all of Our words and thoughts and put some order to it! Now ! Time is fleeting!!

We love and honor your battle, but only you can win or lose it! There will be many other chances (expressions) but at what level would you like to leave this one? You have the power to rise to great spiritual heights if you will simply acknowledge Our presence in your life in an appropriate and personal way!

Go for it and it will reward you handsomely!!!!

Love, God, and all of your family in spirit!!!

PAY ATTENTION TO WHO YOU ARE NOW

You listen, but only with one ear. The other is forever tuned to your mind's dialogue, which takes you nowhere. Despite how far you've come, you remain powerless to claim the fruits of your journey. Reach out and present your gifts to those who would hear you. They are waiting to hear My words, but fearful that they are not worthy.

You have proved yourself worthy through your actions and (will again through the) actions that I require of you now. This now, and all of your future nows, are woven of the same fabric. Time. Endless time. Meaningless time, unless it is used in My service, and for the greater good of the universe.

Pay attention to who you are now, and then stay in the now at all times. This means all of your actions be in accordance with who you really are. The soul of Marshall Jerome Rosenkrantz resides in the body of Jerry Marshall, a fabrication conceived of as an escape from an intolerable series of events, but a fabrication that need not remain permanent. Your vision is clear and has been building over the course of the years. It isn't just the notes that you hear and choose to play. It is the thoughts that you have the opportunity to put into action. Get back to Marshall Jerome Rosenkrantz-land, and become again that searching, creative soul you have always been.

THIS TASK IS IN NO WAY YOURS ALONE

When my voice is heard by all, none can do harm. It is to this end that you have been chosen, chosen to spread this thought. You have the ability to hear and think and feel and care. As such you have the human power to express my desires and needs to mankind. Be assured that this task is in no way yours alone (witness the countless manifestations in the publishing industry). You can spot my emissaries from a mile off. Each and every one has come through the fires of emotional, psychological, and spiritual growth similar to yours.

Your mind runs with fear as to the amount of time you have. Use your time wisely, and it's endless. Use it frivolously and it only seems endless. The choice is yours.

Go in peace and follow your heart. Play your horn, sing with joy from your heart – a heart that is capable of touching other hearts. Use your gifts, for they are many and varied. Your problem has always been a fear of commitment. Fear is the absence of Love, and Love is where and what you are.

You hear us at many times, but you are so busy working at spirit that you overcome the initial transmission and then work hard at physical manifestations. We are always available, but only to a discerning ear. Count yourself fortunate that at this moment in earth time you are coming to the light. This is a trip of endless duration.

Now is all you have. And now is when you have all that you have. Use it in God's name and do His work on earth as you have done so often in past life times. I could enumerate many of them (you already have an inkling of some), but it's not necessary to know them. What is necessary is to know the power that you have right now. The power of being able to hear me and sense me around you at all times.

WE ARE EVER NEAR TO FILL YOUR VOICE WITH GOD'S WORD

We are as real as anything you have touched. Were you to recall your dream of last night, that too you would see as part of the same reality. All that you are experiencing is a human dream gauged to your soul's learning curve. The more you can adjust appropriately and accomplish those things need to be learned on the earth plane, the higher your ascension will be upon arrival at our plane. Your voice is desperately needed in these times, and we are ever near to fill your voice with God's word.

It is really of no great importance in the long range view of your planet. The worrisome thing is that what you (humanity as a whole) do is now cap1able of affecting the entire universe adversely.

Look how conscious your leaders have become of late when the evidence before them has become overwhelming as to global warming. Do you think you are the first and only civilization to behold such a dire consequence? The Atlantians, and antiquity before them, all had the same opportunities to create Atlantis here on earth, and below the sea. It was only human frailty that led to their destruction. There was no cataclysmic strike of God's will. Why would I destroy all that I have created?

You have opened your ear to Me and taken to your typewriter to write My words. But consider the enormous amount of energy required to move you off the bed, to find paper, and finally to move beyond (all your) hindrances, and go directly to your computer to activate My words. In the past you would have gone directly to your papers and pen and been a ready and willing assistant in My quest for peace on your planet.

You see the journey as few others have been able to discern it. You have your records of your journey of discovery, and you even have your teachers all around you. Do avail yourself of them and move on to Our common goal: the awakening of your planet to the majesty that awaits if they will but listen to the same voice you hear, and that is available to all who would listen.

MY WORD IS THE SAME NOW
AS IT HAS ALWAYS BEEN

It really is that simple. I never tried to complicate things. My Word is the same now as it has always been, and My messengers are from the same source as those throughout the eons. All that changes is the manifestation of the degree of destruction that becomes available and the speed at which eternity can be (ignored) by those who listen only to their own madness.

Forgive Me for going on in this manner but you can well imagine the frustration at not being able to bring about the heaven on earth that I promised so long ago. I cannot do it alone, for there is no separation. We are all in this together. What Yassir Arafat does at any given moment indirectly affects that which Mubarak does, as well as Bush, and so on down the line. All are interconnected by a frail and taut line that weaves its way round the globe in endless turns, and envelops all. Who would have envisioned such a state of affairs years ago when the U S and Russia were the players on the world stage? Now they have laid some of the toys to rest, others take up the battle cry. Over what?

There is more than enough to house, feed, and provide for each and every one of My children, yet look at the world you have created, a world you have made out of a paradise that I had created.

How do We, you and I, save it from itself? All you need do is be who you are. An awakened soul, in contact with God, and willing to serve God in whatever way you can. Begin again a regular program of meditation and awareness to My Presence and become My presence on earth once again.

Remember, this is not Our first time around. It has just been a little harder for you to break the bonds that bound you to your earth's birth. You are now well on your way to seeing the process in total clarity, which is a long step in your evolutionary journey. Keep stepping.

WHY ME, LORD?

Me: *Why me, Lord?*

God: Because you're there and you are listening.

Most people don't even listen. All will be revealed at the proper time. Could you have ever imagined that you would be sitting in conversation with Me one on one? Yet here we are and you can't allow yourself the pleasure of our meetings! You still can't accept your hard earned gift. How many people on earth do you think enjoy the privilege, yet you still can't enjoy it!

You have worked for this moment all of your soul's existence! To be "One with God." Here you are and you look at with it fear and wonder. Why you? Why not?

You can't know of all of your past incarnations and so you can't see the "Chinese Wall" you have climbed. But We can! It's a painting on our walls and it's about to be signed if you can but find the courage to come out and play with Us!

Help us to help others to see the possibilities! You are fully worthy! You are well beyond the need for self-gratification and so, do this for all humanity! The gift is in your hands and just waiting to be opened! Share it, spread it around. Let people know the heights to which they can aspire. It's all available and it's available to all and it can be theirs at the "drop of a hat".

Uncovering the mind and allowing your soul to shine – this is a glorious sight! You would love to see what it is that We see!

Share it! Spread it all over and allow yourself the grandeur that you are.

We love and admire you. Love, God and all who wish you well.

YOU ARE MERELY THE INSTRUMENT OF GOD'S WILL

Sit quietly and do nothing! Nothing needs to be done! It is all being done through you and not by you! Ego must evacuate the premises! The whole premise is that you are merely the instrument of God's will and as such your ego needs to be out of the way and you need to be comfortable being that instrument of God's will. Can you imagine what would occur if your trumpet began to determine what notes to play and how to play them? You wouldn't stand for it for a moment and would probably throw the horn against the wall!

Not so with God's love!

You have free will and the abundance of God's love, and there is no judgment which occurs! When you completely recognize your role as an instrument of God's will and stop trying to manipulate the valves you will find that the blessing will flow accordingly.

Go to your day with naught but love in your heart and all will be as ordained.

Your Loving Father, God

YOU MUST WRITE

Me: Oh Heavenly Father, anoint me with Your love and fill my thoughts with that which You would have me do.

God: Well, said, but unnecessary. All of these words have crossed between Us many times before. It is for you to decipher and put into action. Just as Jesus had his plan of action and responded to His challenges, so must you. Don't consider all of the mundane chores you are presently anticipating. All will be provided for your needs as well as Gail's.

It is for you to put your mind on hold and dedicate your time and energy to get Our words in print and into the marketplace. You must write. Yes, you must write. No Us! We have given you more than enough…and it is not for Us to do your work on Earth. We, each and every soul who is a conscious part of the God force have been through a form of your current state of mind and affairs, and We rose above the petty and mundane in order to Our Lord's work on Earth. It is now your turn! You have more than enough information to fill many books, but your mind is still keeping you locked into old and horrible habits. Note them, and then drop them as quickly as you note them.

Begin to write again. You watched a video of your old shows and marveled at what you wrote and produced. Couldn't even imagine how it all came together. Remember, it wasn't only the words and the music, it was the concept and the staging an the technical imagination. All elements that you brought together with a moment's hesitation.

Yes, We saw the thought cross your creative mind (about rewriting your play and music). It is a good story and one that can be shot in a very professional way without great investment.

Do you see how it works? It is all just pieces of fabric coming together to form a new and different piece of the total fabric which is continually changing. Be a part of the change and don't get stuck in old stuff.

Go to sleep and waken and read My words once again as you have begun to do. I will keep you close to My Heart.

Love, God and all of your guides, too numerous to mention.

God: Sit quietly and do nothing! Nothing needs to be done! It is all being done through you and not by you! Ego must evacuate the premises! The whole premise is that you are merely the instrument of God's will and as such your ego needs to be out of the way and you need to be comfortable being that instrument of God's will. Can you imagine what would occur if your trumpet began to determine what notes to play and how to play them? You wouldn't
stand for it for a moment and would probably throw the horn against the wall!

Not so with God's love!

You have free will and the abundance of God's love and there is no judgment which occurs! When you completely recognize your role as an instrument of God's will and stop trying to manipulate the valves you will find that the blessing will flow accordingly.

Go to your day with naught but love in your heart and all will be as ordained.

Your Loving Father, God

YOU MAY, AT LAST, BE BREAKING OUT
OF THE PRISON YOU HAVE ERECTED

Sit quietly! Get a grip! You hear Us and it's that instantaneous if you are listening. You see the panic you are in right now, and it's as though everything is imploding, at once, upon you! The other way to view it is that you may, at last, be breaking out of the prison you have erected that has kept you from realizing your "self".

That "self" that has tried to crawl out of the locks and bars got a good look at what it has created!! The problem is you still can't lose the ego, which wants to keep you locked into this reality you have created which says: "who am I to have these gifts?"

You chose these gifts and responsibilities going in! You chose all of the obstacles - your parents, your financial position, etc. in order to learn the lessons your soul needed, to clear your karmic path for further growth. You are well on you way, and then your ego creeps back in and dumps everything it has in its arsenal to keep you in check!

Fight!!! Fight for your life! Fight for the realization, and the development of the gifts you came in with! You need to do the work!!!

Stay Aware and Awake! Sing. Sing with joy for your gifts and God's unending and constant love!

I am everywhere for you, in whatever form is necessary! We are the only reality, and the sooner you surrender, the easier the trip will be!

Love, God

IT DOESN'T MATTER WHO
GETS THE MESSAGE

You have come through the fires and are now in the clouds of misunderstanding! Actually, there is no way of understanding for the ways of the earth are beyond understanding! They are too vast and multidimensional and would take up more pages then it's worth to deal with now! Actually this "now" is all We have and so let's deal with it!

It doesn't matter who gets the message! It simply matters that it is gotten out in a universe run amuck!

Your loving Father

STAND YOU MUST!

The time has come to understand the forces arrayed before you! They are strong in their covenant and believe their cause is just! Where it will lead is as a river creating its own bed! A rueful force, with the power of endless droplets propelling it! Where it will lead is anybody's guess! Surely it will have devastating consequences upon those who are not in the stream and stand by the banks and wonder at its course!

It will take inordinate courage to stand in place in the face of such a stream, but stand you must! This is a testing time for mankind, and as you can see, the turning tide will wash over much of all you have ever known!

Keep faith with Me and I will keep faith with you! Come to Me often and walk in My light and those around you will be saved by the light of your understanding! As they say in the biz: This is just a test!

Sleep now and rest, for it will be a trying time!

God, and all of your guides, too numerous to mention.

WORDS FROM THE HOLY SPIRIT

I am here for you my child and all you have to do is request My presence. We are one in God's thought, and you have labored long to reenter the kingdom. Welcome home! Continue on your path and you will find the like spirits who will help to guide you to fruition. Have faith that you have struggled for this morning and remember that I am here for you.

Enjoy your day, but keep a place in your thoughts for Me at all times.

Love, The Holy Spirit

The Newtonian concept of a mechanical worldview is now fast eroding with the advent of Einstein, Heisenberg, *et al.* And the Quantum theories join together mankind in a relationship of truly universal brotherhood. The realization that we are not our bodies, nor our minds, but that consciousness which can, if awareness is present, witness the entire process. Recognize the part you're playing by rote, and bring a greater peace into this new, yet old consciousness that you are an integral part of.

We know you understand all of this intellectually, and it is our desire to have it become more of an experiential knowledge.

Go in peace and know you have our blessing and are never out of view.

Love, the Holy Spirit

WE ARE NOT OUR BODIES

Don't fear. The dizziness is just a new elevation of consciousness. A lightness of self. It's as though you are a balloon which is rising as it drops its weights. It is only when we can lift all of these weights that we can truly soar to the heaven, which is of this existence, but hidden to the eyes of those who are weighted down with a reality of their own making (creation), manufactured by the ego's needs and kept in place by the ego's machinations.

It is this sense that mankind has existed under. A Newtonian concept of a mechanical world view, which is now fast eroding with the advent of Einstein, Heisenberg, *et al*. And the quantum theories, which joins together mankind in a relationship as a truly universal brotherhood. The realization that we are not our bodies, nor our minds, but that consciousness which can, if awareness is present, witness the entire process, much like a movie, recognize the part you're playing by rote, and bring you a greater peace in this new, yet old, consciousness that you are an integral part of!

We know you understand all of this intellectually, and it is our desire to have it become more of an experiential knowledge. It is an individual growth process and each to his own time and place! Go in peace and know you have our blessing and are never out of view.

Love, The Holy Spirit

FOREVER IN MY CARE

Me: I call upon the Holy Spirit to guide me along my path.

Holy Spirit: You are under my guidance and have been forever. It is only now that you have become aware of my voice and the love we share. All you have to do is ask, and I will gladly fulfill your desires. This is an abundant universe, and it's yours to partake of. But you have to make the contact and come from a place of desire for that contact.

Sit quietly and ask for the Holy Spirit to enter and grant your request. It's as simple as that.

WORDS FROM JESUS

Jesus, your all time savior. I say that without hesitation because I serve as the Master's voice on earth, and We are all the Master's energy on the earth plane.

There is no capitalization of my (name) when relating to me, only of God when relating to all there is.

You are caught on the horns of a dilemma, and it is as it should be! Hurt by the manipulative feminine energy that has been your curse, as well as your catalyst! It has always been thus down through the ages, and each time you come closer to a realization of the true dynamics of the exercise!

You came to the fray with clear intent! You were able to subdue your ego's need for expression when you realized that your ego was not a player in this moment of time! It was a wonderful test and you passed with flying colors!

SURRENDER

If I had to have been in an ego mind during my playlet, just imagine what hurt would have really meant! It is nothing more than surrender! Always surrender! Nothing more than your first surrender at Malaila's so short a time ago! We are talking about a relative time span here, and since it is all happening at the same time none of it really matters in the reality your persona is currently experiencing! It's something like a traveling minstrel show and everyone gets to play out all of the roles necessary to complete the curriculum! If you can contain your hurt to a point of reconciliation with the lesson learned, then the moment will stand you in good stead as you move on and up the spiral, the never ending spirals!

AS FOR YOU, I LOVE YOU!

As for you, I love you! Just to watch your struggle is to see the whole picture in one snapshot! Let go and let love! It's only the briefest moment in time, and it can be gone or it can linger on and become all of the Hal and Jimmy show all over again! That was a major forgiveness act! This is a very minor one and as we move on the acts become smaller and smaller and easier and easier to see and release!

You have passed another "mother" test with almost flying colors! It will be interesting to see if you are able to release totally or you will have to pass on some of your frustration to others in the form of guilt and recriminations. All of it is just grist for the mill and the choices are all yours!

We love you and honor your struggle! Keep up the good fight!

Love, Jesus and all of your merry band

BEGINNING AGAIN

Okay, let's begin again. That's all there really is. New beginnings. At every turn of your existence, each moment is new. It is filled with all possibilities. That is the way life is as well.

Now it's time for you to fulfill Our needs of you. You are in the perfect spot. Surrounded by love and respect and without the familiar sights and sounds to remind you of all the madness you have left behind.

Go to your day in love and with those you love.

Jesus, God, All who hold you in the highest regard.

CHAPTER IV

CHANNELING JOHN LENNON

I | 25 | 95

ONAN: "STAND BY FOR LENIN"

Now, "STAND BY FOR LENNON". You have called and I have come! I know of your great love for me and I am in your debt! It is interesting how you got there, and it's another of your well-documented journey of discovery. As you can imagine my journey was certainly mind boggling for me, since I had a very rebellious streak in me to start. Ego was a huge factor in my growth because I had to really fight to overcome it, and there were so many elements out of my control which worked against my ascension!

You are blessed with Gail, a woman of peace and love and understanding. Yoko was my blessing, but it was not always with peace and love and understanding! Culture shock was a prime motivator in many of our moments, but were it not for the shocks I would have never known the growth! If anyone would have told me the direction my life would have taken I would have laughed till I was silly! Yet, as I look from this perch it is interesting to realize how prophetic my unconscious and innocent remark, about being better known than Jesus, was at that time! What with all the publicity attendant to the Beatles and such can you imagine what publicity

Jesus would have generated?!

It is of great comfort to be able to communicate with consciousness of all persuasions and see the interest and the sincerity of individuals striving to be apart from the madness of ego. Keep your fight alive and share the learning with all you can, for that is what your part of the puzzle is all about!

Love, Lennon, John to you!!!

1 | 6 | 95

ONAN: "I FEEL PRIVILEGED TO PARTICIPATE IN YOUR DISCUSSIONS WITH JOHN"

He (John) is a very high soul indeed, and much has been my fortune to be in his company. As on Earth, as it is in heaven. There are those of us who choose to reincarnate in order to uplift those spirits who are not aware of the "light," or of the opportunity, while on the earth plane, to avail themselves of the higher power they possess intuitively. John is certainly one whose mission it was to bring that "light" to the earth plane in this century, and the method he chose was one in which mass communication served its highest purpose and touched a maximum of souls, yours included. Coming from your background and musical tastes, you had to make a quantum leap, as Chopra would say (he, too, is a very high teacher and leading the way into the 21st century). Yes, I speak in terms of your earth times, because to ignore the earth concepts would be to deny us the ability to relate to you in a common manner. As you have been learning, there is no such thing as time as you know it, but that is for a higher moment in your learning curve to fully comprehend.

For now, I will leave you in the hands of one who can teach you much.

Farewell, my friend,

Love.

THE OVERWHELMING SCOPE

This is John, and a wise decision you have made because the ego is violently trying to intercept and interrupt our communication right now. You are doing the work necessary to put all of the material in the right place so that you can edit it down, but I see that your ego is fighting you all of the way. I will come and help you through this process.

It isn't necessary to withhold all of the references between you and me because in reality, there is no separation. You and I are one, and your efforts – and mine – are coming from the same place and going to the same place, in the name of our Father, God!

Don't be overwhelmed by the scope of it, as you have been on previous occasions, as this is what it is that you have been searching for, for most of your life. We will be able to accomplish this, so let's just go ahead and deal with it page by page, and I will try to help you, in editing, so that it will reflect the information that we are embarked upon to convey to a general population.

The material that you have taken down so far has been 100% accurate as to my words to you, and so we are operating in truth and with our highest purpose in mind. Know that, and then rest assured that all will follow as it should. I wish that I could get to your computer and do the editing for you for that would simplify the process greatly, but perhaps you will sense my approval or disapproval as you weed through all – all of the material. It is a huge task that we ask of you but it is certainly within your ability and sensitivity to accomplish. Just listen for the small voice inside your head at all times and you will know that I am there and with you at all times. Go ahead with the work now as you have been doing and we will continue the editing.

Thank you, Love, John

THE EGO

There is nothing wrong with an ego that is in the service of the higher self and comes from right-minded thinking. It is like operating a vehicle or your computer. The problem is that it has been in control and has had its own way for a long period of time. It still sees its function in terms of what it has known in the past. You are creating a great chasm for the ego to cross, and it doesn't like to take giant steps like that with ease.

WAKE UP TIME

Is it at last really wake up time or another false alarm? You have been reading over years and years of fears upon fears! Of movement and retreat, commitment and sloth! It has been a rough night of the soul but you do persevere! I'll give you that!

Look at my travels and travail! Once I got the message it was no longer possible to ignore, or bury under a pseudo lifestyle! Lord knows I drifted in and out of the madness for some time, but through it all I know what had to done and went about it in a quite dramatic fashion! Yoko by my side and trusting my new-found knowledge because instinctively she was attracted to the same source, but from another direction!

John, you have seen me in action, as well as inaction! What role is mine to play? I'm so fearful of exposure to my "real" self personally, as well as exposing it to the outside world!

That's just it! There is no outside and inside! It's all one and wide open to change and motion! You simply are not in motion, just reeling from one memory to another, even with the knowledge that you have acquired you still fall into dreams of old stuff! If you want to spend precious time digging around in that cesspool leave Us out of it! We are trying to invite you in to an endless ocean of pure love which will envelop you, nourish you, and allow you to sustain, so that you will have the courage to proclaim your sainthood!

Hallelujah! You actually wrote it all down without a backward glance! Before, every time We approached the concept you ran like a banshee! Sure, the fun starts now! Wait till you proclaim yourself and see what comes of it! If you thought dreams of old jobs were bad, wait till you see the fears of old friends manifest! They will be merciless, just as Jesus watched as he gazed down from His cross! All about Him were neighbors, classmates, playmates, and relatives, all ready to chastise him, in the way of the times, for simply proclaiming what it is you are now understanding and experiencing!

They have no clue, nor do they allow for any clues to enter because they have been seduced by this "reality" to the point of completely denying the possibility of any other "reality"! It is all "One" reality and all are a part of, and in, it!

You need to carry that message through, for there are others who need to hear it from someone who has traveled a like course and discovered a hidden land! Can you imagine what Lewis and Clarke endured? What those Indians along the way encountered and had to deal with? All exploring a new horizon!

You have accomplished a similar feat, and now you must go about reporting upon it and sharing it with others who are afraid to leave their familiar shore for the beauty and peace that awaits them should they venture off of their beaten path!

Beaten is an appropriate word since they could just as easily fly freely as you have intuited by your visualization of the operating vehicle of your soul that appeared to you clearly so long ago! All are planets, universes, organisms, whatever term suits you, in a vast arena of like vehicles.

You drifted off, as is your wont, but at least you held on to the tether that ties all together! Eh? A nice line there?

FEAR

Your fears are overwhelming you again. Jerry Marshall, just do it! No fear! No "who am I to have this knowledge?" You are Our representative on earth, and you have a sworn duty to uphold. It supercedes all of your fears and must override them at all costs. Do you think hanging on a cross in Bethlehem is any different than being burned over and over by your own fears? My moments were beautiful, for I knew where I came from and where I was going to.

Your friend,

John, Lennon to you

MY OWN TRIP. "LORD KNOWS I TRIED."

Jerry Marshall, whatever gets you thorough the days and nights, "get back to where you once belonged" (Loretta). Reread and read and let it cast you back into Our net so that you may proclaim yourself in this experience, this lifetime, and lead others to the glory you have rightfully acquired through dint of dedication, desire, determination, and most hard to come by, commitment.

Do you think my trip was a delight? Imagine being in that hotel room with Yoko and all of those hyenas from the press. You know what I was about, but did they? No, all they knew was that they were going to get a shot at an international story, except it wasn't the story we were trying to present. It was all about who and where they were. "Lord knows I tried." (Old punch line)

Your friend, John

THE CONCERT OF A LIFETIME

Here we are in the true "twilight" of your career, and it can be the "concert" of a lifetime!. Nay, of many, many lifetimes, and you sit on it and wait.

Your friend, John

IT'S ABOUT TIME AND STOP KILLING TIME

It's about time, and yes, We're always around! Why do you seem so surprised? This is not a first for Us! You have been falling into old, old patterns and you see what it brings with it! Depression! A sense of worthlessness! And of the other self-destructive attitudes that destroys your creativity and sense of self-worth!

We are glad that you were moved by the book about George (Harrison). His was a commitment made in heaven! I, at least, just skirted around the edges and like George, had my eyes opened by the LSD! True, I had a glance, but my role turned out to be more in keeping with my personality and sense of humor! I just found it incomprehensible for me, a guitar picker from Liverpool, to be the recipient of such a gift, and it scared the shit out of me! As I think on it now, even this is mind boggling given all that I've grown to and expanded to!

You will love it when you get here and We, John, George, Stan, Mathew, Betty, Murray, and all of the loves of your life that brought you to this moment, We all, and I mean all that you can even think of, are once again as one in God's love!

Your friend,

John, Lennon to you

Thank you for taking a moment. You certainly have a way of killing time, and time is all you have! Think of all the lost opportunities as you hold valiantly on to your neurosis. Fear of exposure. With all you know, you, you still can't own it. It's about time, and that's all it's about. Get off of it and get over it! Start writing. Tie together those phrases rolling around in your head. Can't you see how you are blocking out all of the loving thoughts and actions available to you from the depths of understanding. Your ease of understanding and relating to the *Course in Miracles* material you are currently rereading should be some kind of key to understanding the depth of knowledge.

Stop killing time! It's all you have!

John (You note the absence of Love, for it is difficult to watch you blow all that you know because of stuff that should have been long resolved. Be the Savior you are meant to be!)

Love, John

THE CREATIVE FLOW

Get Our work done! Stay focused and open and We will be besides you all the way. We are excited…and you should share that excitement. It is only when the soul is excited that all other aspects of mankind's activities are brought into creative flow.

Can you see the picture in your mind? We can. Stay the course and We will all revel togther on earth as it is in heaven, hallowed be your name, for it is the same as Ours.

John, Murray, God and All who love and admire you

OUR SUPPORT

We are ever here and will step in wherever and whenever we feel it is appropriate! However, this is your trip, your book, your statement, your coming out party! If you thought others had a hard time coming out, you ain't seen nothing yet! You must hold to your experience and honor it at all times, because it is the only thing that's real in your dimension!

It is that which ties all dimensions together and is far too short of humans who are willing to follow their calling and proclaim their truth in the face of all who only know their calling in terms of financial, or power, rewards! Suffice it to say that we believe you are now prepared to do battle and we are behind, above, around, and within you 100% and more!!!

Go to it!! John, Onan, Mother, Dad, brother, nephew and all of your loving guides

CHAPTER V

CHANNELING ALL MY GUIDES

WORDS FROM "ALL"
YOUR PURPOSE IS TO SERVE AS GOD'S LIAISON

Y OU POSSESS VITAL INFORMATION THAT needs to be passed onto the population at large! You were chosen for this mission for just the attributes which are yours naturally. You have put aside ego for the most part, even though it has reared its ugly head in dreams of late, and (you) are anxious to pursue your greater purpose in life. This has been a quest of yours, even before you began to awaken, and if you check through your old writings you will see it formulated time and time again.

Your purpose is to serve as God's liaison! Do not fear the thought is too grandiose for your ego to let pass by, but it is as it is. You need to take the time necessary to put what thoughts you think "you" are thinking on to your computer in an orderly fashion! The picture you are able to see must be shared by a great many others in order for the puzzle to be seen more clearly by the multitude of others who also are searching. Just as Chopra, Dyer, Williamson, Einstien, Bohr, *et al.* were able to see through the fog, so are you able to see a small part of the clarity which is available to all. It is this clarity that will carry those who seek it through to the coming millennium!

You clearly see the madness that abounds every where on your planet: "from the lovely single cell", (*a quote from something I wrote*) growing rampantly in the body of man, and known as cancer, to the cancer on the soul of mankind which is slowly eating at that larger soul with the same intensity. It is time!!!

Put down your thoughts, which are actually our thoughts, since you are clearly a part of the whole, in a cohesive manner! All of the notations which you have underlined and have allowed you to piece those parts together, allowed you the power to see a larger and greater whole! It is imperative that this information be shared in an entertaining manner! Your mind just perceived a way, by seeing the puzzle come together on a computer! A computer game which would allow practitioners the opportunity to seek their own answers in a pre-proscribed "game of chance"! That's all that there is, even though Einstien couldn't believe God would allow this process to be a "game of chance". It is no game!!! He who has the desire to be a part of the Holy Grail must commit to the search on his own terms and in his own time! The key to the search is to be in "joy" and love will find its way!

Trust the process and begin to organize all of your underlines so that you can clearly see the path that you have charted and the shortcuts that are available to others!! All human form is searching for the same thing. "Love is all there is" and it is that love which transcends all other experiences and allows you to feel the God presence in your vibrating soul! You are as a string on God's lyre, being more and more finely tuned to the highest vibration! Allow yourself to experience the gift in a rapturous manner and pass it on to others who are in your vibrational field!!

Me: Who is speaking?

Jerry! It no longer matters who is speaking for there really is no separation other than that which you would create in your mind. We are all but a thought of God, as your are, and as such we spread our light waves in ever expanding circles of energy, touching more and more souls who are beginning to come to the light! Just as you were drawn to the window to see the breaking of the dawn, so too is your concentration in this mode tantamount to bringing in the dawn!

You are part of a new age!! Not crystals and beads and such, as you warned Gail about, but of an awareness and caring and commitment to sharing of your intuitive knowledge, which will help to light up the darkness in each of your areas of concern!! You will be consistently guided and provided for in the manner of your need as you go about God's business on earth!

Have a great day today and begin to function with a clear eye as to your purpose!

Love, All

THE UNDERLYING PRINCIPLES

What are the underlying principles you have been able to discern from all of Our discourses? Let us enumerate them:

1) No separation. This is the guiding principle.
2) There is no God per se. You, each and every living soul, is a God in the making, created by your every choice from the moment of birth to the planet.

We love and honor your struggle, All

DIS-EASE PRECEDES DISEASE

Jerry, Jerry, Jerry! Can't you see the box you have painted yourself into? We have offered you the keys to the kingdom, but your earthly fears have trumped each and every time. We're here and We sense your dis-ease. It is exactly what precedes disease, as you know it. Sense it and reject it and get back to your power base. You know what works for you. Short bursts of sleep and work and then rest and do it again. You know well the history of others with like minds and how efficient they are when they followed the dictates of their own souls. This is what you must do.

Can you not see it? Can you not rise above it? You, who were so strong and courageous in times (expressions) past are now laid low by those fears and powerless to move past them. You have untold gems stored in loose-leaf books. Songs that go unsung. What are you waiting for, as Christopher Fry so eloquently put it? "Will you wake for pity's sake?"

Wake at last to the wonder that you are. Who else hears the beauty that you do? Walsch, Chopra, Dyer, Zukov, and all the ladies like Myss, Northrup, Williamson. A pantheon of listeners, and you are among them 'cept for your overburdening fears. Even your birth mother has implored you to rise above her fears, and here you sit and write Our words, understand Our information, and scribe it all without a moment's difficulty.

Work at it wholeheartedly. We are imploring you. We are trying as best we can to urge you on to glory.

You feel the waves of your body as it reacts to the garbage you have inflicted on it. Gird yourself and charge! The charge of the "light" brigade! No, not soldiers of death, but knowing, caring, and knowledgeable souls carrying the "light" forward.

Charge! Charge into the Valley of Death and resurrect those who are blind to Our beauty and majesty. That's what this is all about, and you are one of the Our generals. Assume your leadership once again.

Your horn! Get to it! It is crying out to you. Your voice is in the same state. You are the one who has left. Come back and reclaim your gift!

We love and admire you, but grow weary of your slothful ways when you surrender to your ego's ploys.

Can you not see what a wonder you are? Can you not simply offer yourself to the universe and let it speak for itself? Yeah or nay. It's as simple as that.

If you were to view the human body's elements as separate and apart, it would be the same as seeing the majesty of the stars and the planets. Each is a part of the whole. In humans – All – each and every cell operates with full knowledge of its own function, as well as its realizations of its part of the whole. When we come to the same understanding of our function as part of the whole – the whole being the universe which we are simply a part of, it will no longer be possible to ignore the fact that our actions have the potential to destroy the organism we are part of.

You can picture it, and now you must make others able to see what you have come to see. Go to your treasures and offer them now.

Love, All your guides, too numerous to mention.

HEALTH

Do not sweat the little losses of awareness as long as consciousness is present to dull the sword of ego's putting it in your face. It's an old trick and has worked on and off for eons. You are now aware of it and its effects upon your existence. Deal with it from a state of consciousness, and all will be well and done.

Love from All

LEARN A NEW INSTRUMENT

You must learn a new instrument — which is you — and how best to project it with sincerity, single purposefulness, and simplicity. It is imperative for you to work assiduously on this point so as to not lose the momentum.

Love, All your guides, too numerous to mention.

TIME AND SPACE

It would be wise to once again create the time (you have already created the space) to create the joy that can envelope you for your remaining time on earth. It will help you to create the financial ease which, in turn, will circulate your talents and accomplishments and fill your life with joy.

ADMONITIONS AND NUCLEAR THREAT

Lock yourself in. Dive in with abandon and dispel the ego that wants its vehicle in tact and in control. Do you want to see a tombstone that says, "Here are the remains of the ego of Jerry Marshall, nee Marshall Jerome Rosenkrantz, who could never ski past the fear." Or, "Here Lies, in scattered ashes, The Man from Fear."

What a waste of time and energy. On your part, as well as Ours! Don't let it end this way! We have vested interest in your success. Ten years of teaching. You have the relative teaching of a Doctorate in Philosophy or Religion, and you are pissing it away.

Write! Write! Right now! We love and admire you, but are swiftly losing patience. Hate to say, "See you the next time around." Just think of having to do it all over again. That's enough to jump start anyone!

What do you think John experienced not so very long ago? Do you think that was a piece of cake? Yet he manifested Our truth in hundreds of ways, all the while still stuck in a mind set of conflicting needs.

Ours are not threats. They are necessary to bring you up sharply. You clearly see the wave of the future of the world. The lines are being clearly drawn, and the forces are beginning to dig their trenches along party lines. Each line is in accord with the thought of their own god and all the concepts that go with it. Do you not see how easy it is to kill in the name of God, the God you all are.

The potential for the atom and nuclear bombs was always there, as is the potential for peace on earth! Our song has never been sung. Such a loving and truthful testament is buried away for 40 years under the debris of your fears. When already?

Love, All of your guides, too numerous to mention

PUT YOUR TRUST IN US

We have a long history together and welcome you back into the fold once again. You have a way of slipping back that astounds Us. How can you slip back in to the madness once you've had a glimpse of who you are and have been over and over again. You have always been a leader of men and women and animals forever. It is your basic nature. Why would you fear such a gift. You are, and always have been, one of the chosen few.

Love, All

YOU HAVE BEEN HERE BEFORE

Of course you've been here before. All of these lesson are repeatable until they sink in and force a change in behavior.

Love from All

YOU HOLD THE CLUES FOR OTHERS

We are very pleased with what is going on as an overview! We say overview because We see all sides of the puzzle as it is being cut and pieced together! Put your trust in Us since We are the orchestrators and you are the players! Without your expertise what would We have to show on your plane?

You hold the clues for others to perceive what is in store for their future! Since there is no future in terms of soul and spirit, or on other planes, it means that you can only play on the arena you currently occupy!

There is plenty of room for self-expression as long as it is clearly understood at the outset, that there is no self to express! All are a part of each other and therefore ego is valueless as We move on to sainthood, without all of the quirkiness of religious order!

Love, All

REVELATION

Know that the ego will do all in its power to break our connection! Scan your readings from the beginning for "universal truths". Establish an instant rapport with those who share your abilities and nurture this closeness for it is the root of the "new "family of man" taking hold on earth, and it is from this evolutionary process that mankind will be "reborn" again!

Jesus, as you know him, will be truly revealed to you who have eyes to see. Do not fear the grandeur of this concept for you have been in His presence throughout your many sojourns.

There is no separation on this plane, even though we still retain an awareness of the individual "moments" spent in "school" on earth!!! They are as thoughts that pass in the night and only serve to heighten our awareness of the "Unity of All," for it is those moments of separation which remind us of the glory of our Godliness and the "Oneness of All"! You can see how the "ripples" grow from those who can touch the "source of their being" and spread the words and concepts and make possible each soul's deliverance!

Sleep well. Love, All

CHAPTER VI

CHANNELING MUSIC

1963

THE JEWISH BOY
CHANNELS A CHRISTMAS SONG

I T WAS CHRISTMAS WEEK, AND Miami Beach was in the throes
of "The Season." All the hotels along Collins Avenue were
thronged with tourists. At the Fontainebleau Hotel, the line to
get into the La Ronde Supper Club, where Tony Martin and
Cyd Charisse were performing, snaked around the magnificent lobby,

I was a trumpet player in the band and, in the hour's intermission
between sets, I took refuge from the throngs in the beautiful terraced
gardens that led to the ocean. There, on a marble bench, I sat and
quietly took in all the splendor. That particular hour made a lifelong
impression on me.

On one of these nights, I felt compelled to write. Hurrying to the
lobby, I got a pen and paper at the front desk and returned to my
sanctuary. Then I sat, prepared to write, but with no idea as to
what. I waited, and "the what" erupted in a torrent of words. I
just wrote everything that came through me down and then read it
back, amazed at its beauty, rhythm and the rhyme. I had not revised
a single word from the unbidden flow. Never had I ever written
anything with such clarity.

When I returned to the bandstand for the start of the second show, I showed the song to one of the other trumpet players. He grinned and said: "No big thing, you're just getting the message."

What message? I wondered. After all, the song's sentiments were easy for him, as an Italian and Catholic, to grasp. But for a Jew from the Bronx, it was could as easily have been a Greek sonnet. Here, read it for yourself and/or listen: You can download the recording I made several years later at: www.

Let's Spread Christmas All Over The Year
And fill our lives with perpetual cheer.
It's not just the presents we get and give,
But His very presence each day that we live.

So fill your hearts full of joy and good cheer,
And sing a song that the whole world can hear.
And share your gifts with those far and near, and
Let's Spread Christmas All Over The Year.

Let's Spread Christmas All Over the Year.
Let church bells peal o'er the world loud and clear for
all men are brothers with one common aim,
The joy of His birth is for all to acclaim.

So heed His word as a guide for your life,
Just love each other, no struggle or strife.
The bells are ringing so lend an ear, and
Let's Spread Christmas All Over The Year.

JOHN CHANNELS A TUNE TO ME

One evening, completely unexpectedly, John told me he wanted me to write down the music for a song. "How do I do that?" I asked, "You play guitar and piano, I play trumpet." "Just listen," he instructed (Of course I'd heard those words before.) Here are notes and lyrics John wrote and which I transcribed. (Later, the pianist Bill Fayne conceived the piano accompaniment which you can hear at:

Can you imagine what it's like
To float among the clouds
Above the maddening miracles you are.

You all are miracles in process
Learning day by day
The wonders of God's great and wondrous ways.
The wonders of God's great and wondrous ways.
Can you conceive of all that matters
And know it matters not
For every waking moment's but a deram.
And if you can imagine that,
Then just imagine this:
All that matters is all a fleeting dream –
The wonders of God's great and wondrous ways.

To hear the song, go to:
http://www.bluehairlady.com/sites/bluehairlady.com/files/LENNON_SONG.mp3

WALT WHITMAN'S THE MYSTIC TRUMPET

After coming upon Walt Whitman's epic poem *The Mystic Trumpet* I was inspired to compose this orchestral piece that so eloquently celebrates the human spirit.

Enjoy the performance,
Part 1 http://www.youtube.com/watch?v=cXj4LWQVA-A
Part 2 http://www.youtube.com/watch?v=Aa859S2KwSw
Part 3 http://www.youtube.com/watch?v=0eUMU2chUFQ

We will get all of Our material earthbound,
and by that I mean bound beneath the covers of a book
which can touch other souls who are
having like experiences!

Perhaps the ultimate motivation is death.
It is actually a life sentence
of the grandest design!

All of your guides, too numerous to mention.

To hear Jerry's CD, "In the Moment," go to:
http://www.emusic.com/listen/#/album/jerry-marshall/in-the-moment/11866158/

www.ingramcontent.com/pod-product-compliance
Lightning Source LLC
Chambersburg PA
CBHW022135080426
42734CB00006B/375